OUTLINE OF THE
U.S. LEGAL SYSTEM

EQUAL JUSTICE UNDER LAW

OUTLINE OF THE

U.S. LEGAL SYSTEM

Bureau of International Information Programs
United States Department of State
http://usinfo.state.gov
2004

U.S. LEGAL SYSTEM

C O N T E N T S

INTRODUCTION
The U.S. Legal System 4

CHAPTER 1
History and Organization of the Federal Judicial System 18

CHAPTER 2
History and Organization of State Judicial Systems 44

CHAPTER 3
Jurisdiction and Policy-Making Boundaries 56

CHAPTER 4
Lawyers, Litigants, and Interest Groups in the Judicial Process 72

CHAPTER 5
The Criminal Court Process 90

CHAPTER 6
The Civil Court Process 118

CHAPTER 7
Federal Judges 140

CHAPTER 8
Implementation and Impact of Judicial Policies 158

The Constitution of the United States 177

Amendments to the Constitution of the United States 192

Glossary 204

Bibliography 212

Index 214

THE U.S. LEGAL SYSTEM

In this scene from an 1856 painting by Junius Brutus Searns, George Washington (standing, right) addresses the Constitutional Convention, whose members drafted and signed the U.S. Constitution on September 17, 1787. The Constitution is the primary source of law in the United States.

Every business day, courts throughout the United States render decisions that together affect many thousands of people. Some affect only the parties to a particular legal action, but others adjudicate rights, benefits, and legal principles that have an impact on virtually all Americans. Inevitably, many Americans may welcome a given ruling while others — sometimes many others — disapprove. All, however, accept the legitimacy of these decisions, and of the courts' role as final interpreter of the law. There can be no more potent demonstration of the trust that Americans place in the rule of law and their confidence in the U.S. legal system.

The pages that follow survey that system. Much of the discussion explains how U.S. courts are organized and how they work. Courts are central to the legal system, but they are not the entire system. Every day across America, federal, state, and local courts interpret laws, adjudicate disputes under laws, and at times even strike down laws as violating the fundamental protections that the Constitution guarantees all Americans. At the same time, millions of Americans transact their day-to-day affairs without turning to the courts. They, too, rely upon the legal system. The young couple purchasing their first home, two businessmen entering into a contract, parents drawing up a will to provide for their children — all require the predictability and enforceable common norms that the rule of law provides and the U.S. legal system guarantees.

This introduction seeks to familiarize readers with the basic structure and vocabulary of American law. Subsequent chapters add detail, and afford a sense of how the U.S. legal system has evolved to meet the needs of a growing nation and its ever more complex economic and social realities.

A FEDERAL LEGAL SYSTEM: Overview

The American legal system has several layers, more possibly than in most other nations. One reason is the division between federal and state law. To understand this, it helps to recall that the United States was founded not as one nation, but as a union of 13 colonies, each claiming independence from the British Crown. The Declaration of Independence (1776) thus spoke of "the good People of these Colonies" but also pronounced that "these United Colonies are, and of Right ought to be, FREE AND INDEPENDENT STATES." The tension between one people and several states is a perennial theme in American legal history. As explained below, the U.S. Constitution (adopted 1787, ratified 1788) began a gradual and at times hotly contested shift of power and legal authority away from the states and toward the federal government. Still, even today states retain substantial authority. Any student of the American legal system must understand how jurisdiction is apportioned between the federal government and the states.

The Constitution fixed many of the boundaries between federal and state law. It also divided federal power among legislative, executive, and judicial branches of government (thus creating a "separation of powers" between each branch and enshrining a system of "checks-and-balances" to prevent any one branch from overwhelming the others), each of which contributes distinctively to the legal system. Within that system, the Constitution delineated the kinds of laws that Congress might pass.

As if this were not sufficiently complex, U.S. law is more than the statutes passed by Congress. In some areas, Congress authorizes administrative agencies to adopt rules that add detail to statutory requirements. And the entire system rests upon the traditional legal principles found in English Common Law. Although both the Constitution and statutory law supersede common law, courts continue to apply unwritten common law principles to fill in the gaps where the Constitution is silent and Congress has not legislated.

SOURCES OF FEDERAL LAW

The United States Constitution

Supremacy of Federal Law

During the period 1781–88, an agreement called the Articles of Confederation governed relations among the 13 states. It established a weak national Congress and left most authority with the states. The Articles made no provision for a federal judiciary, save a maritime court, although each state was enjoined to honor (afford "full faith and credit" to) the rulings of the others' courts.

The drafting and ratification of the Constitution reflected a growing consensus that the federal government needed to be strengthened. The legal system was one of the areas where this was done. Most significant was the "supremacy clause," found in Article VI:

> This Constitution, and the Laws of the United States which shall be made in Pursuance thereof; and all Treaties made, or which shall be made, under the Authority of the United States, shall be the supreme Law of the Land; and the Judges in every State shall be bound thereby, any Thing in the Constitution or Laws of any State to the Contrary notwithstanding.

This paragraph established the first principle of American law: Where the federal Constitution speaks, no state may contradict it. Left unclear was how this prohibition might apply to the federal government itself, and the role of the individual state legal systems in areas not expressly addressed by the new Constitution. Amendments would supply part of the answer, history still more, but even today Americans continue to wrestle with the precise demarcations between the federal and state domains.

Each Branch Plays a Role in the Legal System

While the drafters of the Constitution sought to strengthen the federal government, they feared strengthening it too much. One means of restraining the new regime was to divide it into branches. As James Madison explained in *Federalist No. 51*, "usurpations are guarded against by a division of the government into distinct and separate departments." Each of Madison's "departments," legislative, executive, and judiciary, received a measure of influence over the legal system.

Legislative

The Constitution vests in Congress the power to pass legislation. A proposal considered by Congress is called a *bill*. If a majority of each house of Congress — two-thirds should the President veto it — votes to adopt a bill, it becomes law. Federal laws are known as *statutes*. The *United States Code* is a "codification" of federal statutory law. The *Code* is not itself a law, it merely

The Constitution has vested the power to pass legislation in Congress, here gathered in a joint session for President George W. Bush's budget speech in 2001. The executive power, in turn, is entrusted to the President.

presents the statutes in a logical arrangement. Title 20, for instance, contains the various statutes pertaining to Education, and Title 22 those covering Foreign Relations.

Congress' lawmaking power is limited. More precisely, it is delegated by the American people through the Constitution, which specifies areas where Congress may or may not legislate. Article I, Section 9 of the Constitution forbids Congress from passing certain types of laws. Congress may not, for instance, pass an "ex post facto" law (a law that applies retroactively, or "after the fact"), or levy a tax on exports. Article I, Section 8 lists areas where Congress may legislate. Some of these ("To establish Post Offices") are

Laws passed by one of the 50 state legislatures, such as the New York State Assembly shown above during a roll call, apply only to the citizens of that state or outsiders who reside or do business there.

quite specific but others, most notably, "To regulate Commerce with foreign Nations, and among the several States," are less so. Obviously the power to interpret the less precise delegations is extremely important. Early in the young republic's history, the judiciary branch assumed this role and thus secured an additional and extremely vital role in the U.S. legal system.

Judicial

As with the other branches, the U.S. judiciary possesses only those powers the Constitution delegates. The Constitution extended federal jurisdiction only to certain kinds of disputes. Article III, Section 2 lists them. Two of the most significant are cases involving a question of federal law ("all Cases in Law and Equity, arising under this Constitution, the Laws of the United States, and Treaties made...") and "diversity" cases, or disputes between citizens of two different states. Diversity jurisdiction allows each party to avoid litigating his case before the courts of his adversary's state.

A second judicial power emerged in the Republic's early years. As explained in Chapter 2, the U.S. Supreme Court in the case of *Marbury v. Madison* (1803) interpreted its delegated powers to include the authority to determine whether a statute violated the Constitution and, if it did, to declare such a law invalid. A law may be *unconstitutional* because it violates rights guaranteed to the people by the Constitution, or because Article I did not authorize Congress to pass that kind of legislation.

The power to interpret the constitutional provisions that describe where Congress may legislate is thus very important. Traditionally, Congress has justified many statutes as necessary to regulate "commerce... among the several States," or interstate commerce. This is an elastic concept, difficult to describe with precision. Indeed, one might for nearly any statute devise a plausible tie between its objectives and the regulation of interstate commerce. At times, the judicial branch interpreted the "commerce clause" narrowly. In 1935, for instance, the Supreme Court invalidated a federal law regulating the hours and wages of workers at a New York slaughterhouse because the chickens processed there all were sold to New York butchers and retailers and hence not part of interstate commerce. Soon after this, however, the Supreme Court began to afford President Franklin D. Roosevelt's New Deal programs more latitude, and today the federal courts continue to interpret broadly the commerce power, although not so broadly as to justify any legislation that Congress might pass.

Executive

Article II entrusts to the President of the United States "the executive Power." Under President George Washington (1789–1801), the entire executive branch consisted of the President, Vice President, and the Departments of State, Treasury, War, and Justice. As the nation grew, the executive branch grew with it. Today there are 15 Cabinet-level Departments. Each houses a number of Bureaus, Agencies, and other entities. Still other parts of the executive branch lie outside these Departments. All exercise executive power delegated by the President and thus are responsible ultimately to him.

In some areas, the relationship between the executive and the other two branches is clear. Suppose one or more individuals rob a bank. Congress has passed a statute criminalizing bank robbery (*United States Code*, Title 18, Section 2113*). The Federal Bureau of Investigation (FBI), a bureau within the Department of Justice, would investigate the crime. When it apprehended one or more suspects, a Federal Prosecutor (also Department of Justice) would attempt to prove the suspect's guilt in a trial conducted by a U.S. District Court.

The bank robbery case is a simple one. But as the nation modernized and

---

* Technically, the statute applies only to a bank that is federally chartered, insured, or a member of the Federal Reserve System. Possibly every bank in the United States meets these criteria, but one that did not, and could not be construed as impacting interstate commerce, would not be subject to federal legislation. Federal statutes typically recite a jurisdictional basis: in this case, the federal charter requirement.

Federal and state courts hear two kinds of disputes: civil and criminal. Here an attorney representing landowners in a civil action presents his arguments to the South Dakota Supreme Court.

Left, civil law covers statutes pertaining to marriage and divorce. This couple is being married in this civil ceremony performed by a judge. At right, a judge in Texas. In the past few decades, the U.S. judiciary has expanded to include more women and minorities.

grew, the relationship of the three branches within the legal system evolved to accommodate the more complex issues of industrial and post-industrial society. The role of the executive branch changed most of all. In the bank robbery example, Congress needed little or no special expertise to craft a statute that criminalized bank robbery. Suppose instead that lawmakers wished to ban "dangerous" drugs from the marketplace, or restrict the amount of "unhealthful" pollutants in the air. Congress could, if it chose, specify precise definitions of these terms. Sometimes it does so, but increasingly Congress instead delegates a portion of its authority to administrative agencies housed in the executive branch. The Food and Drug Administration (FDA) thus watches over the purity of the nation's food and pharmaceuticals and the Environmental Protection Agency (EPA) regulates how industries impact the earth, water, and air.

Although agencies possess only powers that Congress delegates by statute, these can be quite substantial. They can include the authority to promulgate rules that define with precision more general statutory terms. A law might proscribe "dangerous" amounts of pollutants in the atmosphere, while an EPA rule defines the substances and amounts of each that would be considered dangerous. Sometimes a statute empowers an agency to investigate violations of its

rules, to adjudicate those violations, and even to assess penalties!

The courts will invalidate a statute that grants an agency too much power. An important statute called the Administrative Procedure Act (*United States Code* Title 5, Section 551, et. seq.) explains the procedures agencies must follow when promulgating rules, judging violations, and imposing penalties. It also lays out how a party can seek judicial review of an agency's decision.

Other Sources of Law

The most obvious sources of American law are the statutes passed by Congress, as supplemented by administrative regulations. Sometimes these demarcate clearly the boundaries of legal and illegal conduct — the bank robbery example again — but no government can promulgate enough law to cover every situation. Fortunately, another body of legal principles and norms helps fill in the gaps, as explained below

Common Law

Where no statute or constitutional provision controls, both federal and state courts often look to the common law, a collection of judicial decisions, customs, and general principles that began centuries ago in England and continues to develop today. In many states, common law continues to hold an important role in contract disputes, as state legislatures have not seen fit to pass statutes covering every possible contractual contingency.

Judicial Precedent

Courts adjudicate alleged violations of and disputes arising under the law. This often requires that they interpret the law. In doing so, courts consider themselves bound by how other courts of equal or superior rank have previously interpreted a law. This is known as the principle of "stare decisis," or simply precedent. It helps to ensure consistency and predictability. Litigants facing unfavorable precedent, or case law, try to distinguish the facts of their particular case from those that produced the earlier decisions.

Sometimes courts interpret the law differently. The Fifth Amendment to the Constitution, for instance, contains a clause that "[n]o person... shall be compelled in any criminal case to be a witness against himself." From time to time, cases arose where an individual would decline to answer a subpoena or otherwise testify on the grounds that his testimony might subject him to criminal prosecution — not in the United States but in another country. Would the self-incrimination clause apply here? The U.S. Court of Appeals for the Second Circuit ruled it did, but the Fourth and Eleventh Circuits held that it did not.* This effectively meant that the law differed depending where in the country a case arose!

Higher-level courts try to resolve these inconsistencies. The Supreme Court of the United States, for instance, often chooses to hear a case when its decision can resolve a division among the Circuit courts. The Supreme Court precedent will control, or apply to all the lower federal courts. In *United States v. Balsys*, 524 U.S. 666 (1998), the Supreme Court ruled that fear of foreign prosecution is beyond the scope of the Self-Incrimination Clause.**

This ruling became the law of the entire nation, including the Second Circuit. Any federal court subsequently facing the issue was bound by the high court ruling in *Balsys*. Circuit court decisions similarly bind all the District Courts within that circuit. *Stare decisis* also applies in the various state court systems. In this way, precedent grows both in volume and explanatory reach.

---

*The U.S. Circuit Court for the Second Circuit is an appellate court that hears appeals from the federal district courts in the states of New York, Connecticut, and Vermont. The Fourth Circuit encompasses Maryland, North Carolina, South Carolina, Virginia, and West Virginia, and the Eleventh Alabama, Georgia, and Florida. For more information on the organization of the federal courts, see chapter 1.

**The numbers in this sentence comprise the *citation* to the *Balsys* decision. They indicate that the Court issued its ruling in the year 1998 and that the decision appears in volume 524 of a series called *United States Reports*, beginning on page 666.

DIFFERENT LAWS; DIFFERENT REMEDIES

Given this growing body of law, it is useful to distinguish among different types of laws and of actions, or lawsuits, brought before the courts and of the remedies the law affords in each type of case.

Civil/Criminal

Courts hear two kinds of disputes: civil and criminal. A civil action involves two or more private parties, at least one of which alleges a violation of a statute or some provision of common law. The party initiating the lawsuit is the plaintiff; his opponent the defendant. A defendant can raise a counterclaim against a plaintiff or a cross-claim against a co-defendant, so long as they are related to the plaintiff's original complaint. Courts prefer to hear in a single lawsuit all the claims arising from a dispute. Business litigations, as for breach of contract, or tort cases, where a party alleges he has been injured by another's negligence or willful misconduct, are civil cases.

While most civil litigations are between private parties, the federal government or a state government is always a party to a criminal action. It prosecutes, in the name of the people, defendants charged with violating laws that prohibit certain conduct as injurious to the public welfare. Two businesses might litigate a civil action for breach of contract, but only the government can charge someone with murder.

The standards of proof and potential penalties also differ. A criminal defendant can be convicted only upon the determination of guilt "beyond a reasonable doubt." In a civil case, the plaintiff need only show a "preponderance of evidence," a weaker formulation that essentially means "more likely than not." A convicted criminal can be imprisoned, but the losing party in a civil case is liable only for legal or equitable remedies, as explained below.

Legal and Equitable Remedies

The U.S. legal system affords a wide but not unlimited range of remedies. The criminal statutes typically list for a given offense the range of fines or prison time a court may impose. Other parts of the criminal code may in some jurisdictions allow stiffer penalties for repeat offenders. Punishment for the most serious offenses, or felonies, is more severe than for misdemeanors.

In civil actions, most American courts are authorized to choose among legal and equitable remedies. The distinction means less today than in the past but is still worth understanding. In 13th century England, "courts of law" were authorized to decree monetary remedies only. If a defendant's breach of contract cost the plaintiff £50, such a court could order the defendant to pay that sum to the plaintiff. These damages were sufficient in many instances, but not in others, such as a contract for the sale of a rare artwork or a specific parcel of land. During the 13th and 14th centuries, "courts of equity" were formed. These tribunals fashioned equitable remedies like specific performance, which compelled parties to perform their obligations, rather than merely forcing them to pay damages for the injury caused by their nonperformance. By the 19th century, most American jurisdictions had eliminated the distinction between law and equity. Today, with rare exceptions, U.S. courts can award either legal or equitable remedies as the situation requires.

One famous example illustrates the differences between civil and criminal law, and the remedies that each can offer. The state of California charged the former football star O.J. Simpson with murder. Had Simpson been convicted, he would have been imprisoned. He was not convicted, however, as the jury ruled the prosecution failed to prove Simpson's guilt beyond a reasonable doubt. Afterwards, Mrs. Simpson's family sued Simpson for wrongful death, a civil action. The jury in this case determined that a preponderance of the evidence demonstrated Simpson's responsibility for the death of his wife. It ordered Simpson to pay money damages — a legal remedy — to the plaintiffs.

The U.S. Constitution explicitly sets out that large parts of the U.S. legal system remain under the control of the individual states. Here, Cook County, Illinois, Circuit Court Judge William H. Haddad, left, and Illinois Supreme Court Justice Thomas R. Fitzgerald.

THE ROLE OF STATE LAW IN THE FEDERAL SYSTEM

The Constitution specifically forbade the states from adopting certain kinds of laws (entering into treaties with foreign nations, coining money). Also, the Article VI Supremacy Clause barred state laws that contradicted either the Constitution or federal law. Even so, large parts of the legal system remained under state control. The Constitution had carefully specified the areas where Congress might enact legislation. The

Family law remains almost exclusively a state matter. Here, Attorney Catherine Smith argues a case involving a child caregiver's rights in front of the state Supreme Court in Olympia, Washington. Chief Justice Gerry L. Alexander, right, and Justice Charles Z. Smith listen.

Tenth Amendment to the Constitution (1791) made explicit that state law would control elsewhere: "The powers not delegated to the United States by the Constitution, nor prohibited by it to the States, are reserved to the States, respectively, or to the people."

There nonetheless remained considerable tension between the federal government and the states — over slavery, and ultimately over the right of a state to leave the federal union. The civil conflict of 1861–65 resolved both disputes. It also produced new restrictions on the state role within the legal system: Under the Fourteenth Amendment (1868), "No State shall... deprive any person of life, liberty or property, without due process of law; nor deny to any person within its jurisdiction the equal protection of the laws." This amendment greatly expanded the federal courts' ability to invalidate state laws. *Brown v. Board of Education* (1954), which forbade racial segregation in the Arkansas state school system, relied upon this "equal protection clause."

Beginning in the mid-20th century, a number of the trends outlined above — the rise of the administrative state, a more forceful and expansive judicial interpretation of due process and equal protection, and a similar expansion of Congress' power to regulate commerce — combined to enhance the federal role within the legal system. Even so, much of that system remains within the state domain. While no state may deny a citizen any right guaranteed by the federal Constitution, many interpret their own constitutions as bestowing even more generous rights and privileges. State courts applying state law continue to decide most contractual disputes. The same is true of most criminal cases, and of civil tort actions. Family law, including such matters as marriage and divorce, is almost exclusively a state matter. For most Americans most of the time, the legal system means the police officers and courts of their own state, or of the various municipalities and other political subdivisions within that state.

This introduction offers a mere thumbnail sketch of the legal system. The remainder of the volume affords greater detail, flavor, and understanding. Chapters 1 and 2 describe respectively how the federal and state court systems have been organized, while Chapter 3 explains at length the complex question of jurisdiction. The chapter necessarily delineates the borders between the federal and state courts but it also explores the question of who may sue, and of the kinds of cases courts will hear. Chapter 4 expands the focus from the courts to the groups who appear before them. The practice of law in the United States is studied, and the typical litigants described. The chapter also explains the role played by interest groups that press particular cases to advance their social and political agendas. Chapter 5 details how the courts handle criminal cases while Chapter 6 turns the focus to civil actions. Chapter 7 describes how federal judges are selected. The final chapter explores how certain judicial decisions — those of higher courts especially — can themselves amount to a form of policymaking and thus further entwine the judiciary in a complex relationship with the legislative and executive branches.

— By Michael Jay Friedman

Michael Jay Friedman is a Program Officer in the U.S. Department of State, Bureau of International Information Programs. He holds a Ph.D. in American History from the University of Pennsylvania and a J.D. degree from Georgetown University Law Center.

HISTORY
AND
ORGANIZATION
OF
THE
FEDERAL
JUDICIAL
SYSTEM

Chief Justice John Marshall, who headed the U.S. Supreme Court from 1801 to 1835, in a portrait by Alonzo Chappel. Marshall's dominance of the Court allowed him to initiate major changes, including adopting the practice of the Court handing down a single opinion.

One of the most important, most interesting, and, possibly, most confusing features of the judiciary in the United States is the dual court system; that is, each level of government (state and national) has its own set of courts. Thus, there is a separate court system for each state, one for the District of Columbia, and one for the federal government. Some legal problems are resolved entirely in the state courts, whereas others are handled entirely in the federal courts. Still others may receive attention from both sets of tribunals, which sometimes causes friction. The federal courts are discussed in this chapter and the state courts in chapter 2.

THE HISTORICAL CONTEXT

Prior to the adoption of the Constitution, the United States was governed by the Articles of Confederation. Under the Articles, almost all functions of the national government were vested in a single-chamber legislature called Congress. There was no separation of executive and legislative powers.

The absence of a national judiciary was considered a major weakness of the Articles of Confederation. Consequently, the delegates gathered at the Constitutional Convention in Philadelphia in 1787 expressed widespread agreement that a national judiciary should be established. A good deal of disagreement arose, however, on the specific form that the judicial branch should take.

The Constitutional Convention and Article III

The first proposal presented to the Constitutional Convention was the Virginia Plan, which would have set up both a Supreme Court and inferior federal courts. Opponents of the Virginia Plan responded with the New Jersey Plan, which called for the creation of a single federal supreme tribunal. Supporters of the New Jersey Plan were especially disturbed by the idea of lower federal courts. They argued that the state courts could hear all cases in the first instance and that a right of appeal to the Supreme Court would be sufficient to protect national rights and provide uniform judgments throughout the country.

The conflict between the states' rights advocates and the nationalists was resolved by one of the many compromises that characterized the Constitutional Convention. The compromise is found in Article III of the Constitution, which begins, "The judicial Power of the United States, shall be vested in one supreme Court, and in such inferior Courts as the Congress may from time to time ordain and establish."

The Judiciary Act of 1789

Once the Constitution was ratified, action on the federal judiciary came quickly. When the new Congress convened in 1789, its first major concern was judicial organization. Discussion of Senate Bill 1 involved

THE UNITED STATES COURT SYSTEM

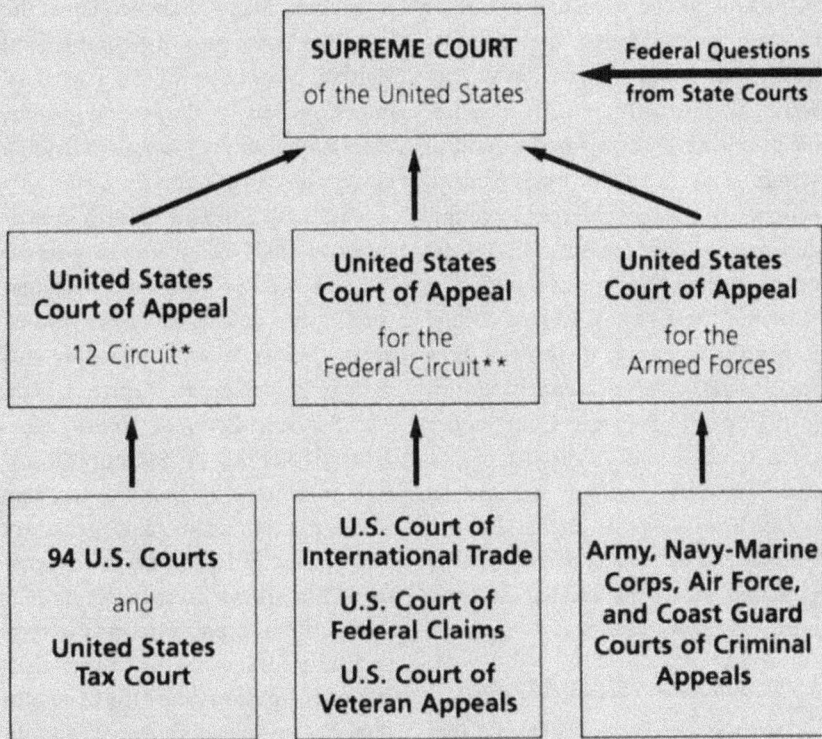

```
                    ┌─────────────────────┐
                    │   SUPREME COURT     │◄──── Federal Questions
                    │ of the United States│      from State Courts
                    └─────────────────────┘
```

United States Court of Appeal 12 Circuit*	United States Court of Appeal for the Federal Circuit**	United States Court of Appeal for the Armed Forces
94 U.S. Courts and United States Tax Court	U.S. Court of International Trade U.S. Court of Federal Claims U.S. Court of Veteran Appeals	Army, Navy-Marine Corps, Air Force, and Coast Guard Courts of Criminal Appeals

* The 12 regional Courts of Appeals also receive cases from a number of federal agencies.

** The Court of Appeals for the Federal Circuit also receives cases from the International Trade Commission, the Merit Systems Protection Board, the Patent and Trademark Office, and the Board of Contract Appeals.

many of the same participants and arguments as were involved in the Constitutional Convention's debates on the judiciary. Once again, the question was whether lower federal courts should be created at all or whether federal claims should first be heard in state courts. Attempts to resolve this controversy split Congress into two distinct groups.

One group, which believed that federal law should be adjudicated in the state courts first and by the U.S. Supreme Court only on appeal, expressed the fear that the new government would destroy the rights of the states. The other group of legislators, suspicious of the parochial prejudice of state courts, feared that litigants from other states and other countries would be dealt with unjustly. This latter group naturally favored a judicial system that included lower federal courts. The law that emerged from this debate, the Judiciary Act of 1789, set up a judicial system composed of a Supreme Court, consisting of a chief justice and five associate justices; three circuit courts, each comprising two justices of the Supreme Court and a district judge; and 13 district courts, each presided over by one district judge. The power to create inferior federal courts, then, was immediately exercised. Congress created not one but two sets of lower courts.

THE U.S. SUPREME COURT

Supreme Court Justice Charles Evans Hughes wrote in *The Supreme Court of the United States* (1966) that the Court "is distinctly American in conception and function, and owes little to prior judicial institutions." To understand what the framers of the Constitution envisioned for the Court, another American concept must be considered: the federal form of government. The Founders provided for both a national government and state governments; the courts of the states were to be bound by federal laws. However, final

interpretation of federal laws could not be left to a state court and certainly not to several state tribunals, whose judgments might disagree. Thus, the Supreme Court must interpret federal legislation. Another of the Founders' intentions was for the federal government to act directly upon individual citizens as well as upon the states.

Given the Supreme Court's importance to the U.S. system of government, it was perhaps inevitable that the Court would evoke great controversy. Charles Warren, a leading student of the Supreme Court, said in *The Supreme Court in United States History:* "Nothing in the Court's history is more striking than the fact that while its significant and necessary place in the Federal form of Government has always been recognized by thoughtful and patriotic men, nevertheless, no branch of the Government and no institution under the Constitution has sustained more continuous attack or reached its present position after more vigorous opposition."

The Court's First Decade

George Washington, the first president of the United States, established two important traditions when he appointed the first Supreme Court justices. First, he began the practice of naming to the Court those with whom he was politically compatible. Washington, the only president ever to have an opportunity to appoint the entire federal judiciary, filled federal judge-

Geographical Boundaries of U.S. Courts of Appeals and U.S. District Courts

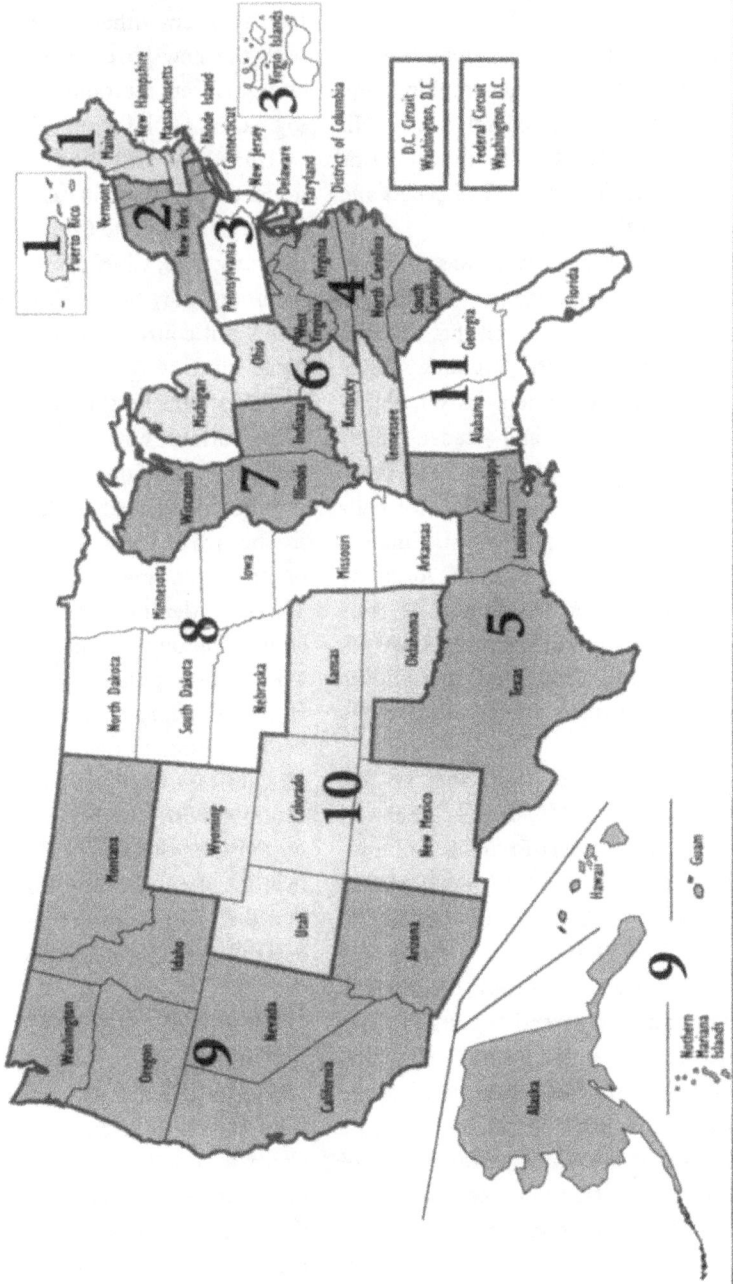

ships, without exception, with faithful members of the Federalist Party. Second, Washington's appointees offered roughly equal geographic representation on the federal courts. His first six appointees to the Supreme Court included three Northerners and three Southerners.

The chief justiceship was the most important appointment Washington made. The president felt that the man to head the first Supreme Court should be an eminent lawyer, statesman, executive, and leader. Many names were presented to Washington, and at least one person formally applied for the position. Ultimately, Washington settled upon John Jay of New York. Although only 44 years old, Jay had experience as a lawyer, a judge, and a diplomat. In addition, he was the main drafter of his state's first constitution.

The Supreme Court met for the first time on Monday, February 1, 1790, in the Royal Exchange, a building located in the Wall Street section of New York City, and its first session lasted just 10 days. During this period the Court selected a clerk, chose a seal, and admitted several lawyers to practice before it in the future. There were, of course, no cases to be decided; the Court did not rule on a single case during its first three years. In spite of this insignificant and abbreviated beginning, Charles Warren wrote, "The New York and the Philadelphia newspapers described the proceedings of this first session of the Court more fully than any other event connected with the new government; and their accounts were reproduced in the leading papers of all the states."

During its first decade the Court decided only about 50 cases. Given the scarcity of Supreme Court business in the early days, Chief Justice Jay's contributions may be traced primarily to his circuit court decisions and his judicial conduct.

Perhaps the most important of Jay's contributions, however, was his insistence that the Supreme Court could not provide legal advice for the executive branch in the form of an advisory opinion. Jay was asked by Treasury Secretary Alexander Hamilton to issue an opinion on the constitutionality of a resolution passed by the Virginia House of Representatives, and President Washington asked Jay for advice on questions relating to his Neutrality Proclamation. In both instances, Jay's response was a firm "No," because Article III of the Constitution provides that the Court is to decide only cases pertaining to actual controversies.

The Impact of Chief Justice Marshall

John Marshall served as chief justice from 1801 to 1835 and dominated the Court to a degree unmatched by any other justice. Marshall's dominance of the Court enabled him to initiate major changes in the way opinions were presented. Prior to his tenure, the justices ordinarily wrote separate opinions (called "seriatim" opinions – Latin for "one after the other") in major cases. Under Marshall's stewardship, the Court adopted the practice of handing down a single opinion. Marshall's goal was to keep dissension to a minimum. Arguing that dissent undermined the Court's authority, he tried to persuade the justices to settle their differences privately and then present a united front to the public. Marshall also used his powers to involve the Court in the policy-making process. Early in his tenure as chief justice, for example, the Court asserted its power to declare an act of Congress unconstitutional, in *Marbury v. Madison* (1803).

This case had its beginnings in the presidential election of 1800, when Thomas Jefferson defeated John Adams in his bid for reelection. Before leaving office in March 1801, however, Adams and the lame-duck Federalist Congress created several new federal judgeships. To fill these new positions Adams nominated, and the Senate confirmed, loyal Federalists. In addition, Adams named his outgoing secretary of state, John Marshall, to be the new chief justice of the Supreme Court.

As secretary of state it had been Marshall's job to deliver the commissions of the newly appointed judges. Time ran out, however, and 17 of the commissions were not delivered before Jefferson's inauguration. The new president ordered his secretary of state, James Madison, not to deliver the remaining commissions. One of the disappointed nominees was William Marbury. He and three of his colleagues, all confirmed as justices of the peace for the District of Columbia, decided to ask the Supreme Court to force Madison to deliver their commissions. They relied upon Section 13 of the Judiciary Act of 1789, which granted the Supreme Court the authority to issue *writs of mandamus* — court orders commanding a public official to perform an official, nondiscretionary duty.

The case placed Marshall in a predicament. Some suggested that he disqualify himself because of his earlier involvement as secretary of state. There was also the question of the Court's power. If Marshall were to grant the writ, Madison (under Jefferson's orders) would be almost certain to refuse to deliver the commissions. The Supreme Court would then be powerless to enforce its order. However, if Marshall refused to grant the writ, Jefferson would win by default.

The decision Marshall fashioned from this seemingly impossible predicament was evidence of sheer genius. He declared Section 13 of the Judiciary Act of 1789 unconstitutional because it granted original jurisdiction to the Supreme Court in excess of that specified in Article III of the Constitution. Thus the Court's power to review and determine the constitutionality of acts of Congress was established. This decision is rightly seen as one of the single most important decisions the Supreme Court has ever handed down. A few years later the Court also claimed the right of judicial review over actions of state legislatures; during Marshall's tenure it overturned more than a dozen state laws on constitutional grounds.

The Changing Issue Emphasis of the Supreme Court

Until approximately 1865 the legal relationship between the national and state governments, or cases of federalism, dominated the Court's docket. John Marshall believed in a strong national government and did not hesitate to restrict state policies that interfered with its activities. A case in point is *Gibbons v. Ogden* (1824), in which the Court overturned a state monopoly over steamboat transportation on the ground that it interfered with national control over interstate commerce. Another good example of Marshall's use of the Court to expand the federal government's powers came in *McCulloch v. Maryland* (1819), in which the chief justice held that the Constitution permitted Congress to establish a national bank. The Court's insistence on a strong national government did not significantly diminish after Marshall's death. Roger Taney, who succeeded Marshall as chief justice, served from 1836 to

1864. Although the Court's position during this period was not as uniformly favorable to the federal government, the Taney Court did not reverse the Marshall Court's direction.

During the period 1865-1937 issues of economic regulation dominated the Court's docket. The shift in emphasis from federalism to economic regulation was brought on by a growing number of national and state laws aimed at monitoring business activities. As such laws increased, so did the number of cases challenging their constitutionality. Early in this period the Court's position on regulation was mixed, but by the 1920s the bench had become quite hostile toward government regulatory policy. Federal regulations were generally overturned on the ground that they were unsupported by constitutional grants of power to Congress, whereas state laws were thrown out mainly as violations of economic rights protected by the Fourteenth Amendment.

Since 1937 the Supreme Court has focused on civil liberties concerns — in particular, the constitutional guarantees of freedom of expression and freedom of religion. In addition, an increasing number of cases have dealt with procedural rights of criminal defendants. Finally, the Court has decided a great number of cases concerning equal treatment by the government of racial minorities and other disadvantaged groups.

The Supreme Court as a Policy Maker

The Supreme Court's role as a policy maker derives from the fact that it interprets the law. Public policy issues come before the Court in the form of legal disputes that must be resolved.

An excellent example may be found in the area of racial equality. In the late 1880s many states enacted laws requiring the separation of African Americans and whites in public facilities. In 1890, for instance, Louisiana enacted a law requiring separate but equal railroad accommodations for African Americans and whites. A challenge came two years later. Homer Plessy, who was one-eighth black, protested against the Louisiana law by refusing to move from a seat in the white car of a train traveling from New Orleans to Covington, Louisiana. Arrested and charged with violating the statute, Plessy contended that the law was unconstitutional. The U.S. Supreme Court, in *Plessy v. Ferguson* (1896), upheld the Louisiana statute. Thus the Court established the "separate-but-equal" policy that was to reign for about 60 years. During this period many states required that the races sit in different areas of buses, trains, terminals, and theaters; use different restrooms; and drink from different water fountains. African Americans were sometimes excluded from restaurants and public libraries. Perhaps most important, African American students often had to attend inferior schools.

Separation of the races in public schools was contested in the famous case *Brown v. Board of Education* (1954). Parents of African American schoolchildren claimed that state laws requiring or permitting segregation deprived them of equal protection of the laws under the Fourteenth Amendment. The Supreme Court ruled that separate educational facilities are inherently unequal and, therefore, segregation constitutes a denial of equal protection. In the Brown decision the Court laid to rest the separate-but-equal doctrine and established a policy of desegregated public schools.

In an average year the Court decides, with signed opinions, between 80 and 90 cases. Thousands of other cases are disposed of with less than the full treatment. Thus the Court deals at length with a very select set of policy issues that have varied throughout the Court's history. In a democracy, broad matters of public policy are presumed to be left to the elected representatives of the people — not to judicial appointees with life terms. Thus, in principle U.S. judges are not supposed to make policy. However, in practice judges cannot help but make policy to some extent.

The Supreme Court, however, differs from legislative and executive policy makers. Especially important is the fact that the Court has no self-starting device. The justices must wait for problems to be brought to them; there can be no judicial policy making if there is no litigation. The president and members of Congress have no such constraints. Moreover, even the most assertive Supreme Court is limited to some extent by the actions of other policy makers, such as lower-court judges, Congress, and the president. The Court depends upon others to implement or carry out its decisions.

The Supreme Court as Final Arbiter

The Supreme Court has both original and appellate jurisdiction. Original jurisdiction means that a court has the power to hear a case for the first time. Appellate jurisdiction means that a higher court has the authority to review cases originally decided by a lower court. The Supreme Court is overwhelmingly an appellate court since most of its time is devoted to reviewing decisions of lower courts. It is the highest appellate tribunal in the country. As such, it has the final word in the interpretation of the Constitution, acts of legislative bodies, and treaties — unless the Court's decision is altered by a constitutional amendment or, in some instances, by an act of Congress.

Since 1925 a device known as "certiorari" has allowed the Supreme Court to exercise discretion in deciding which cases it should review. Under this method a person may request Supreme Court review of a lower court decision; then the justices

determine whether the request should be granted. If review is granted, the Court issues a writ of certiorari, which is an order to the lower court to send up a complete record of the case. When certiorari is denied, the decision of the lower court stands.

The Supreme Court at Work

The formal session of the Supreme Court lasts from the first Monday in October until the business of the term is completed, usually in late June or July. Since 1935 the Supreme Court has had its own building in Washington, D.C. The imposing five-story marble building has the words "Equal Justice Under Law" carved above the entrance. It stands across the street from the U.S. Capitol. Formal sessions of the Court are held in a large courtroom that seats 300 people. At the front of the courtroom is the bench where the justices are seated. When the Court is in session, the chief justice, followed by the eight associate justices in order of seniority, enters through the purple draperies behind the bench and takes a seat. Seats are arranged according to seniority with the chief justice in the center, the senior associate justice on the chief justice's right, the second-ranking associate justice on the left, and continuing alternately in declining order of seniority. Near the courtroom are the conference room where the justices decide cases and the chambers that contain offices for the justices and their staffs.

The U.S. Supreme Court Building, with the words "Equal Justice Under Law" carved above the entrance.

The Court's term is divided into sittings of approximately two weeks each, during which it meets in open session and holds internal conferences, and recesses, during which the justices work behind closed doors as they consider cases and write opinions. The 80 to 90 cases per term that receive the Court's full treatment follow a fairly routine pattern.

Oral Argument. Oral arguments are generally scheduled on Monday through Wednesday during the sittings. The sessions run from 10:00 a.m. until noon and from 1:00 until 3:00 p.m. Because the procedure is not a trial or the original hearing of a case, no jury is assembled and no witnesses are called. Instead, the two opposing attorneys present their arguments to the justices. The general practice is to allow 30 minutes for each side, although the Court may decide that additional time is necessary. The Court can normally hear four cases in one day. Attorneys presenting oral arguments are frequently interrupted with questions from the justices. The oral argument is considered very impor-

The nine justices of the present U.S. Supreme Court are shown above. Seated, from left to right: Associate Justices Antonin Scalia and John Paul Stevens; Chief Justice William Renhquist; Associate Justices Sandra Day O'Connor and Anthony Kennedy. Standing, left to right: Associate Justices Ruth Bader Ginsburg, David Souter, Clarence Thomas, and Stephen Breyer.

tant by both attorneys and justices because it is the only stage in the process that allows such personal exchanges.

The Conference. On Fridays preceding the two-week sittings the Court holds conferences; during sittings it holds conferences on Wednesday afternoon and all day Friday. At the Wednesday meeting the justices discuss the cases argued on Monday. At the Friday conference they discuss the cases that were argued on Tuesday and Wednesday, plus any other matters that need to be considered. The most important of these other matters are the certiorari petitions.

Prior to the Friday conference each justice is given a list of the cases that will be discussed. The conference begins at about 9:30 or 10:00 a.m. and runs until 5:30 or 6:00 p.m. As the justices enter the conference room they shake hands and take their seats around a rectangular table. They meet behind locked doors, and no official record is kept of the discussions. The chief justice presides over the conference and offers an opinion first in each case. The other justices follow in descending order of seniority.

A quorum for a decision on a case is six members; obtaining a quorum is seldom difficult. Cases are sometimes decided by fewer than nine justices because of vacancies, illnesses, or non-participation resulting from possible conflicts of interest. Supreme Court decisions are made by a majority vote. In case of a tie the lower-court decision is upheld.

Opinion Writing. After a tentative decision has been reached in conference, the next step is to assign the Court's opinion to an individual justice. The chief justice, if voting with the majority, either writes the opinion or assigns it to another justice who voted with the majority. When the chief justice votes with the minority, the most senior justice in the majority makes the assignment.

After the conference the justice who will write the Court's opinion begins work on an initial draft. Other justices may work on the case by writing alternative opinions. The completed opinion is circulated to justices in both the majority and the minority groups. The writer seeks to persuade justices originally in the minority to change their votes, and to keep his or her majority group intact. A bargaining process occurs, and the wording of the opinion may be changed in order to satisfy other justices or obtain their support. A deep division in the Court makes it difficult to achieve a clear, coherent opinion and may even result in a shift in votes or in another justice's opinion becoming the Court's official ruling.

In most cases a single opinion does obtain majority support, although few rulings are unanimous. Those who disagree with the opinion of the Court are said to dissent. A dissent does not have to be accompanied by an opinion; in recent years, however, it usually has been. Whenever more than one justice dissents, each may write an opinion or all may join in a single opinion.

On occasion a justice will agree with the Court's decision but differ in his or her reason for reaching that conclusion. Such a justice may write what is called a concurring opinion. An opinion labeled "concurring and dissenting" agrees with part of a Court ruling but disagrees with other parts. Finally, the Court occasionally issues a per curiam opinion — an unsigned opinion that is usually quite brief. Such opinions are often used when the Court accepts the case for review but gives it less than full treatment. For example, it may decide the case without benefit of oral argument and issue a per curiam opinion to explain the disposition of the case.

THE U.S. COURTS OF APPEALS

The courts of appeals receive less media coverage than the Supreme Court, but they are very important in the U.S. judicial system. Considering that the Supreme Court hands down decisions with full opinions in only 80 to 90 cases each year, it is apparent that the courts of appeals are the courts of last resort for most appeals in the federal court system.

Circuit Courts: 1789-1891

The Judiciary Act of 1789 created three circuit courts (courts of appeals), each composed of two justices of the Supreme Court and a district judge. The circuit court was to hold two sessions each year in each district within the circuit. The district judge became primarily responsible for establishing the circuit court's workload. The two Supreme Court justices then came into the local area and participated in the cases. This practice tended to give a local rather than national focus to the circuit courts.

The circuit court system was regarded from the beginning as unsatisfactory, especially by Supreme Court justices, who objected to the traveling imposed upon them. Attorney General Edmund Randolph and President Washington urged relief for the Supreme Court justices. Congress made a slight change in 1793 by altering the circuit court organization to include only one Supreme Court justice and one district judge. In the closing days of President John Adams's administration in 1801, Congress eliminated circuit riding by the Supreme Court justices, authorized the appointment of 16 new circuit judges, and greatly extended the jurisdiction of the lower courts.

The new administration of Thomas Jefferson strongly opposed this action, and Congress repealed it. The Circuit Court Act of 1802 restored circuit riding by Supreme Court justices and expanded the number of circuits. However, the legislation allowed the circuit court to be presided over by a single district judge. Such a change may seem slight, but it proved to be of great importance. Increasingly, the district judges began to assume responsibility for both district and circuit courts. In practice, then, original and appellate jurisdiction were both in the hands of the district judges.

The next major step in the development of the courts of appeals did not come until 1869, when Congress approved a measure that authorized the appointment of nine new circuit judges and reduced the Supreme Court justices' circuit court duty to one term every two years. Still, the High Court was flooded with cases because there were no limitations on the right of appeal to the Supreme Court.

The Courts of Appeals: 1891 to the Present

On March 3, 1891, the Evarts Act was signed into law, creating new courts known as circuit courts of appeals. These new tribunals were to hear most of the appeals from district courts. The old circuit courts, which had existed since 1789, also remained. The new circuit court of appeals was to consist of one circuit judge, one circuit court of appeals judge, one

The courts of appeals review cases appealed from federal district courts. Above, Chief Judge John M. Walker, Jr., U.S. Court of Appeals for the Second Circuit, left, administers the oath of office to Barrington D. Parker, Jr., right, as a judge for the same court.

district judge, and a Supreme Court justice. Two judges constituted a quorum in these new courts.

Following passage of the Evarts Act, the federal judiciary had two trial tribunals: district courts and circuit courts. It also had two appellate tribunals: circuit courts of appeals and the Supreme Court. Most appeals of trial decisions were to go to the circuit court of appeals, although the act also allowed direct review in some instances by the Supreme Court. In short, creation of the circuit courts of appeals released the Supreme Court from many petty types of cases.

Appeals could still be made, but the High Court would now have much greater control over its own workload. Much of its former caseload was thus shifted to the two lower levels of the federal judiciary.

The next step in the evolution of the courts of appeals came in 1911. In that year Congress passed legislation abolishing the old circuit courts, which had no appellate jurisdiction and frequently duplicated the functions of district courts.

Today the intermediate appellate tribunals are officially known as courts of appeals, but they continue to be referred to colloquially as circuit courts. There are now 12 regional courts of appeals, staffed by 179 authorized courts of appeals judges. The courts of appeals are responsible for reviewing cases appealed from federal district courts (and in some cases from administrative agencies) within the boundaries of the circuit. A specialized appellate court came into existence in 1982 when Congress established the Federal Circuit, a jurisdictional rather than a geographic circuit.

The Review Function of the Courts of Appeals

Most of the cases reviewed by the courts of appeals originate in the federal district courts. Litigants disappointed with the lower-court decision may appeal the case to the court of appeals of the circuit in which the federal district court is located. The appellate courts have also been given authority to review the decisions of certain administrative agencies.

Because the courts of appeals have no control over which cases are brought to them, they deal with both routine and highly important matters. At one end of the spectrum are frivolous appeals or claims that have no substance and little or no chance for success. At the other end of the spectrum are the cases that raise major questions of public policy and evoke strong disagreement. Decisions by the courts of appeals in such cases are likely to establish policy for society as a whole, not just for the specific litigants. Civil liberties, reapportionment, religion, and education cases provide good examples of the kinds of disputes that may affect all citizens.

There are two purposes of review in the courts of appeals. The first is error correction. Judges in the various circuits are called upon to monitor the performance of federal district courts and federal agencies and to supervise their application and interpretation of national and state laws. In doing so, the courts of appeals do not seek out new factual evidence, but instead examine the record of the lower court for errors. In the process of correcting errors the courts of appeals also settle disputes and enforce national law.

The second function is sorting out and developing those few cases worthy of Supreme Court review. The circuit judges tackle the legal issues earlier than the Supreme Court justices and may help shape what they consider review-worthy claims. Judicial scholars have found that appealed cases often differ in their second hearing from their first.

The Courts of Appeals as Policy Makers

The Supreme Court's role as a policy maker derives from the fact that it interprets the law, and the same holds true for the courts of appeals. The scope of the courts of appeals' policy-making role takes on added importance, given that they are the courts of last resort in the vast majority of cases.

As an illustration of the far-reaching impact of circuit court judges, consider the decision in a case involving the Fifth Circuit. For several years the University of Texas Law School (as well as many other law schools across the country) had been granting preference to African American and Mexican American applicants to increase the enrollment of minority students. This practice was challenged in a federal district court on the ground that it discriminated against white and nonpreferred minority applicants in violation of the Fourteenth Amendment. On March 18, 1996, a panel of Fifth Circuit judges ruled in *Hopwood v. Texas* that the Fourteenth Amendment does not permit the school to discriminate in this way and that the law school may not use race as a factor in law school admissions. The U.S. Supreme Court denied a petition for a writ of certiorari in the case, thus leaving it the law of the land in Texas, Louisiana, and Mississippi, the states comprising the Fifth Circuit. Although it may technically be true that only schools in the Fifth Circuit are affected by the ruling, an editorial in *The National Law Journal* indicates otherwise, noting that

U.S. courts — both at the level of the Appeals Courts and, in several instances, the Supreme Court — often settle passionately contested issues such as affirmative action in higher education.

while some "might argue that *Hopwood*'s impact is limited to three states in the South..., the truth is that across the country law school (and other) deans, fearing similar litigation, are scrambling to come up with an alternative to affirmative action."

The Courts of Appeals at Work

The courts of appeals do not have the same degree of discretion as the Supreme Court to decide whether to accept a case. Still, circuit judges have developed methods for using their time as efficiently as possible.

Screening. During the screening stage the judges decide whether to give an appeal a full review or to dispose of it in some other way. The docket may be reduced to some extent by consolidating similar claims into single cases, a process that also results in a uniform decision. In deciding which cases can be disposed of without oral argument, the courts of appeals increasingly rely on law clerks or staff attorneys. These court personnel read petitions and briefs and then submit recommendations to the judges. As a result, many cases are disposed of without reaching the oral argument stage.

Three-Judge Panels. Those cases given the full treatment are normally considered by panels of three judges rather than by all the judges in the circuit. This means that several cases can be heard at the same time by different three-judge panels, often sitting in different cities throughout the circuit.

En Banc Proceedings. Occasionally, different three-judge panels within the same circuit may reach conflicting decisions in similar cases. To resolve such conflicts and to promote circuit unanimity, federal statutes provide for an "en banc" (Old French for high seat) procedure in which all the circuit's judges sit together on a panel and decide a case. The exception to this general rule occurs in the large Ninth Circuit where assembling all the judges becomes too cumbersome. There, en banc panels normally consist of 11 judges. The en banc procedure may also be used when the case concerns an issue of extraordinary importance.

Oral Argument. Cases that have survived the screening process and have not been settled by the litigants are scheduled for oral argument. Attorneys for each side are given a short amount of time (as little as 10 minutes) to discuss the points made in their written briefs and to answer questions from the judges.

The Decision. Following the oral argument, the judges may confer briefly and, if they are in agreement, may announce their decision immediately. Otherwise, a decision will be announced only after the judges confer at greater length. Following the conference, some decisions will be announced with a brief order or per curiam opinion of the court. A small portion of decisions will be accompanied by a longer, signed opinion and perhaps even dissenting and concurring opinions. Recent years have seen a general decrease in the number of published opinions, although circuits vary in their practices.

U.S. DISTRICT COURTS

The U.S. district courts represent the basic point of input for the federal judicial system. Although some cases are later taken to a court of appeals or perhaps even to the Supreme Court, most federal cases never move beyond the U.S. trial courts. In terms of sheer numbers of cases handled, the district courts are the workhorses of the federal judiciary. However, their importance extends beyond simply disposing of a large number of cases.

The First District Courts

Congress made the decision to create a national network of federal trial courts when it passed the Judiciary Act of 1789. Section 2 of the act established 13 district courts by making each of the 11 states then in the Union a district, and by making the parts of Massachusetts and Virginia that were to become Maine and Kentucky into separate districts. That organizational scheme established the practice, which still exists, of honoring state boundary lines in drawing districts.

The First District Judges

Each federal district court was to be presided over by a single judge who resided in the district. As soon as this became known, President Washington began receiving letters from individuals desiring appointment to the various judgeships. Many asked members of Congress or Vice President John Adams to recommend them to President Washington. Personal applications were not necessarily successful and were not the only way in which names came to the president's attention. Harry Innes, for example, was not an applicant for the Kentucky judgeship but received it after being recommended by a member of Congress from his state.

As new states came into the Union, additional district courts were created. The additions, along with resignations, gave Washington an opportunity to offer judgeships to 33 people. All of the judges he appointed were members of the bar, and all but seven had state or local legal experience as judges, prosecutors, or attorneys general. Presidents have continued to appoint lawyers with public service backgrounds to the federal bench.

Present Organization of the District Courts

As the country grew, new district courts were created. Eventually, Congress began to divide some states into more than one district. California, New York, and Texas have the most, with four each. Other than consistently honoring state lines, the organization of district constituencies appears to follow no rational plan. Size and population vary widely from district to district. Over the years, a court was added for the District of Columbia, and several territories have been served by district courts. There are now U.S. district courts serving the 50 states, the District of Columbia, Guam, Puerto Rico, the Virgin Islands, and the Northern Mariana Islands.

The original district courts were each assigned one judge. With the growth in population and litigation, Congress has periodically had to add judges to most of the districts. The Federal Judgeship Act of 1990 created 74 new district judgeships, bringing the current total to 649. Today all districts have more than one judge; the Southern District of New York, which includes Manhattan and the Bronx, currently has 28 judges and is thus the largest. Because each federal district court is normally presided over by a single judge, several trials may be in session within the district at any given time.

The District Courts as Trial Courts

Congress established the district courts as the trial courts of the federal judicial system and gave them original jurisdiction over virtually all cases. They are the only federal courts in which attorneys examine and cross-examine witnesses. The factual record is thus established at this level. Subsequent appeals of the trial court decision focus on correcting errors rather than on reconstructing the facts.

The task of determining the facts in a case often falls to a jury, a group of citizens from the community who serve as impartial arbiters of the facts and apply the law to the facts. The Constitution guarantees the right to a jury trial in criminal cases in the Sixth Amendment and the same right in civil cases in the Seventh Amendment. The right can be waived, however, in which case the judge becomes the arbiter both of questions of fact and of matters of law. Such trials are referred to as bench trials.

Two types of juries are associated with federal district courts. The grand jury is a group of men and women convened to determine whether there is probable cause to believe that a person has committed the federal crime of which he or she has been accused. Grand jurors meet periodically to hear charges brought by the U.S. attorney. Petit jurors are chosen at random from the community to hear evidence and determine whether a defendant in a civil trial has liability or whether a defendant in a criminal trial is guilty or not guilty. Federal rules call for 12 jurors in criminal cases but permit fewer in civil cases. The federal district courts generally use six-person juries in civil cases.

Trial courts are viewed as engaging primarily in norm enforcement, whereas appellate courts are seen as having greater opportunity to make policy. Norm enforcement is closely tied to the administration of justice, because all nations develop standards considered essential to a just and orderly society. Societal norms are embodied in statutes, administrative regulations, prior court decisions, and community traditions. Criminal statutes, for example, incorporate concepts of acceptable and unacceptable behavior into law. A judge deciding a case concerning an alleged violation of that law is practicing norm enforcement. Because cases of this type rarely allow the judge to escape the strict restraints of legal and procedural requirements, he or she has little chance to make new law or develop new policy. In civil cases, too, judges are often confined to norm enforcement, because such litigation generally arises from a private dispute whose outcome is of interest only to the parties in the suit.

The district courts also play a policy-making role, however. As Americans have become more litigation-conscious, disputes that were once resolved informally are now more likely to be decided in a court of law. The courts find themselves increasingly involved in domains once considered private. What does this mean for the federal district courts? According to one study, "These new areas of judicial involvement tend to be relatively free of clear, precise appellate court and

legislative guidelines; and as a consequence the opportunity for trial court jurists to write on a clean slate, that is, to make policy, is formidable."

CONSTITUTIONAL COURTS AND LEGISLATIVE COURTS

The Judiciary Act of 1789 established the three levels of the federal court system in existence today. Periodically, however, Congress has exercised its power, based on Article III and Article I of the Constitution, to create other federal courts. Courts established under Article III are known as constitutional courts and those created under Article I are called legislative courts. The Supreme Court, courts of appeals, and federal district courts are constitutional courts. Legislative courts include the U.S. Court of Military Appeals, the United States Tax Court, and the Court of Veterans Appeals.

Legislative courts, unlike their constitutional counterparts, often have administrative and quasi-legislative as well as judicial duties. Another difference is that legislative courts are often created for the express purpose of helping to administer a specific congressional statute. Constitutional courts, on the other hand, are tribunals established to handle litigation.

Finally, the constitutional and legislative courts vary in their degree of independence from the other two branches of government. Article III (constitutional court) judges serve during a period of good behavior, or what amounts to life tenure. Because Article I (legislative court) judges have no constitutional guarantee of good-behavior tenure, Congress may set specific terms of office for them. In sum, the constitutional courts have a greater degree of independence from the other two branches of government than the legislative courts.

ADMINISTRATIVE AND STAFF SUPPORT IN THE FEDERAL JUDICIARY

Although judges are the most visible actors in the judicial system, a large supporting cast is also at work. Their efforts are necessary to perform the tasks for which judges are unskilled or unsuited, or for which they simply do not have adequate time. Some members of the support team, such as law clerks, may work specifically for one judge. Others — for example, U.S. magistrate judges — are assigned to a particular court. Still others may be employees of an agency, such as the Administrative Office of the United States Courts, that serves the entire judicial system.

U.S. Magistrate Judges

In an effort to help federal district judges deal with increased workloads, Congress in 1968 created a system of magistrate judges that responds to each district court's specific needs and circumstances. Magistrate judges are appointed by the judges of the district

court for eight-year terms of office, although they can be removed before the expiration of the term for "good cause." Within guidelines set by the Congress, the judges in each district court establish the duties and responsibilities of their magistrate judges. The legislation permits a magistrate judge, with the consent of the involved parties, to conduct all proceedings in a jury or nonjury civil matter and enter a judgment in the case and to conduct a trial of persons accused of misdemeanors (less serious offenses than felonies) committed within the district, provided the defendants consent. Because the decision to delegate responsibilities to a magistrate judge is still made by the district judge, however, a magistrate judge's participation in the processing of cases may be more narrow than that permitted by statute.

Law Clerks

The first use of law clerks by an American judge is generally traced to Horace Gray of Massachusetts. In the summer of 1875, while serving as chief justice of the Massachusetts Supreme Court, he employed, at his own expense, a highly ranked new graduate of the Harvard Law School. Each year, he employed a new clerk from Harvard. When Gray was appointed to the U.S. Supreme Court in 1882, he brought a law clerk with him to the nation's highest court.

Justice Gray's successor on the High Court was Oliver Wendell

Holmes, who also adopted the practice of annually hiring honor graduates of Harvard Law School as his clerks. When William Howard Taft, a former law professor at Yale, became chief justice, he secured a new law clerk annually from the dean of the Yale Law School. Harlan Fiske Stone, former dean of the Columbia Law School, joined the Court in 1925 and made it his practice to hire a Columbia graduate each year.

Since these early beginnings there has been a steady growth in the use of law clerks by all federal courts. More than 2,000 law clerks now work for federal judges, and more than 600 serve bankruptcy judges and U.S. magistrate judges. In addition to the law clerks hired by individual judges, all appellate courts and some district courts hire staff law clerks who serve the entire court.

A law clerk's duties vary according to the preferences of the judge for whom he or she works. They also vary according to the type of court. Law clerks for federal district judges often serve primarily as research assistants. They spend a good deal of time examining the various motions filed in civil and criminal cases. They review each motion, noting the issues and the positions of the parties involved, then research important points raised in the motions and prepare written memorandums for the judges. Because their work is devoted to the earliest stages of the litigation process, they may have a substantial amount of contact with attorneys and witnesses. Law clerks at this level may be involved in the initial drafting of opinions.

At the appellate level, the law clerk becomes involved in a case first by researching the issues of law and fact presented by an appeal. The courts of appeals do not have the same discretion to accept or reject a case that the Supreme Court has, and they use certain screening devices to differentiate between cases that can be handled quickly and those that require more time and effort. Law clerks are an integral part of this screening process.

A number of cases are scheduled for oral argument, and the clerk may be called upon to assist the judge in preparing for it. Intensive analysis of the record by judges prior to oral argument is not always possible. They seldom have time to do more than scan pertinent portions of the record called to their attention by law clerks.

Once a decision has been reached by an appellate court, the law clerk frequently participates in writing the order that accompanies the decision. The clerk's participation generally consists of drafting a preliminary opinion or order pursuant to the judge's directions. A law clerk may also be asked to edit or check citations (references to a statute, precedent-setting case, or legal textbook, in a brief or argument in court) in an opinion written by the judge.

The work of the law clerk for a Supreme Court justice roughly parallels that of a clerk in the other appellate courts. Clerks play an indispensable role in helping justices decide which cases should be heard. At the suggestion of Justice Lewis F. Powell, Jr., in 1972, a majority of the Court's members began to participate in a "certpool"; the justices pool their clerks, divide up all filings, and circulate a single clerk's certiorari memo to all those participating in the pool. The memo summarizes the facts of the case, the questions of law presented, and the recommended course of action — that is, whether the case should be granted a full hearing, denied, or dismissed.

Once the justices have voted to hear a case, the law clerks, like their counterparts in the courts of appeals, prepare bench memorandums that the justices may use during oral argument. Finally, law clerks for Supreme Court justices, like those who serve courts of appeals judges, help to draft opinions.

Administrative Office of the U.S. Courts

The administration of the federal judicial system as a whole is managed by the Administrative Office of the U.S. Courts. Since its creation in 1939 it has handled everything from distributing supplies to negotiating with other government agencies for court accommodations in federal buildings to maintaining judicial personnel records and collecting data on cases in the federal courts.

The Administrative Office also serves the Judicial Conference of the United States, the central administrative policy-making organization of the federal judicial system. In addition to providing statistical information to the conference's many committees, the Administrative Office acts as a reception center and clearinghouse for information and proposals directed to the Judicial Conference. The office also acts as liaison for both the federal judicial system and the Judicial Conference, serving as advocate for the judiciary in its dealings with Congress, the executive branch, professional groups, and the general public. Especially important is its representative role before Congress where, along with concerned judges, it presents the judiciary's budget proposals, requests for additional judgeships, suggestions for changes in court rules, and other key measures.

The Federal Judicial Center

The Federal Judicial Center, created in 1967, is the federal courts' agency for continuing education and research. Its duties fall generally into three categories: conducting research on the federal courts, making recommendations to improve the administration and management of the federal courts, and developing educational and training programs for personnel of the judicial branch.

Since its inception, judges have benefited from orientation sessions and other educational programs put on by the Federal Judicial Center. In recent years, magistrate judges, bankruptcy judges, and administrative personnel have also been the recipients of educational programs. The Federal Judicial Center's extensive use of videos and satellite technology allows it to reach large numbers of people.

FEDERAL COURT WORKLOAD

The workload of the courts is heavy for all three levels of the federal judiciary — U.S. district courts, courts of appeals, and the Supreme Court.

For fiscal year 2002 slightly more than 340,000 cases were commenced in the federal district courts. Criminal filings alone have risen 43 percent since 1993.

In 1995, 50,072 appeals were filed in one of the regional circuit courts. This figure increased every year, to a high of 60,847 appeals in 2003. However, the number of appeals terminated by the courts of appeals has also been steadily increasing, from 49,805 in 1995 to 56,586 in 2002.

The overall caseload of the Supreme Court is large by historical standards; there were 8,255 cases on the docket for the 2002 term. The Supreme Court, however, has discretion to decide which cases merit its full attention. As a result, the number of cases argued before the Court has declined rather dramatically over the years. In the 2002 term only 84 cases were argued and 79 were disposed of in 71 signed opinions.   ෧

HISTORY AND ORGANIZATION OF STATE JUDICIAL SYSTEMS

Although the organization of state courts can be confusing, there is no doubt about their importance: They handle far more cases than those decided by federal tribunals. Here, a painting depicting the State of Florida Supreme Court Building in Tallahassee.

Even prior to the Articles of Confederation and the writing of the U.S. Constitution in 1787, the colonies, as sovereign entities, already had written constitutions. Thus, the development of state court systems can be traced from the colonial period to the present.

HISTORICAL DEVELOPMENT OF STATE COURTS

No two states are exactly alike when it comes to the organization of courts. Each state is free to adopt any organizational scheme it chooses, create as many courts as it wishes, name those courts whatever it pleases, and establish their jurisdiction as it sees fit. Thus, the organization of state courts does not necessarily resemble the clear-cut, three-tier system found at the federal level. For instance, in the federal system the trial courts are called district courts and the appellate tribunals are known as circuit courts. However, in well over a dozen states the circuit courts are trial courts. Several other states use the term superior court for their major trial courts. Perhaps the most bewildering situation is found in New York, where the major trial courts are known as supreme courts.

Although confusion surrounds the organization of state courts, no doubt exists about their importance. Because statutory law is more extensive in the states than at the federal level, covering everything from the most basic personal relationships to the state's most important public policies, the state courts handle a wide variety of cases, and the number of cases litigated annually in the state courts far exceeds those decided in the federal tribunals.

The Colonial Period

During the colonial period, political power was concentrated in the hands of the governor appointed by the king of England. Because the governors performed executive, legislative, and judicial functions, an elaborate court system was not necessary.

The lowest level of the colonial judiciary consisted of local judges called justices of the peace or magistrates. They were appointed by the colony's governor. At the next level in the system were the county courts, the general trial courts for the colonies. Appeals from all courts were taken to the highest level — the governor and his council. Grand and petit juries were also introduced during this period and remain prominent features of the state judicial systems.

By the early 18th century the legal profession had begun to change. Lawyers trained in the English Inns of Court became more numerous, and as a consequence colonial court procedures were slowly replaced by more sophisticated English common law.

Early State Courts

Following the American Revolution (1775-83), the powers of the government were not only taken over by legislative bodies but also greatly reduced. The former colonists were not eager to see the development of a large, independent judiciary given that many of them harbored a distrust of lawyers and the common law. The state legislatures carefully watched the courts and in some instances removed judges or abolished specific courts because of unpopular decisions.

Increasingly, a distrust of the judiciary developed as courts declared legislative actions unconstitutional. Conflicts between legislatures and judges, often stemming from opposing interests, became more prominent. Legislators seemed more responsive to policies that favored debtors, whereas courts generally reflected the views of

creditors. These differences were important because "out of this conflict over legislative and judicial power...the courts gradually emerged as an independent political institution," according to David W. Neubauer in *America's Courts and the Criminal Justice System.*

The FRAME of the

GOVERNMENT

OF THE

Province of Pennsilvania

IN

AMERICA

Together with certain

LAWS

Agreed upon in England

BY THE

GOVERNOUR

AND

Divers FREE-MEN of the aforesaid

PROVINCE

To be further Explained and Confirmed there by the first Provincial Council and General Assembly that shall be held, if they see meet.

Printed in the Year MDCLXXXII.

REDUCED FAC-SIMILE OF TITLE OF "THE FRAME OF GOVERNMENT."

The colonial period helped establish important legal principles. Left, prominent lawyer Andrew Hamilton's defense of newspaper printer Johann Peter Zenger in 1735 proved a landmark on the road to protecting freedom of the press. Above, a 1682 woodcut of "The Frame of the Government of the Province of Pennsylvania," which included laws agreed upon by the governor and "free men of the aforesaid province."

Modern State Courts

From the Civil War (1861-65) to the early 20th century, the state courts were beset by other problems. Increasing industrialization and the rapid growth of urban areas created new types of legal disputes and resulted in longer and more complex court cases. The state court systems, largely fashioned to handle the problems of a rural, agrarian society, were faced with a crisis of backlogs as they struggled to adjust.

One response was to create new courts to handle the increased volume of cases. Often, courts were piled on top of each other. Another strategy was the addition of new courts with jurisdiction over a specific geographic area. Still another response was to create specialized courts to handle one particular type of case. Small claims courts, juvenile courts, and domestic relations courts, for example, became increasingly prominent.

The largely unplanned expansion of state and local courts to meet specific needs led to a situation many have referred to as fragmentation. A multiplicity of trial courts was only one aspect of fragmentation, however. Many courts had very narrow jurisdiction. Furthermore, the jurisdictions of the various courts often overlapped.

Early in the 20th century, people began to speak out against the fragmentation in the state court systems. The program of reforms that emerged in response is generally known as the court unification movement. The first well-known legal scholar to speak out in favor of court unification was Roscoe Pound, dean of the Harvard Law School. Pound and others called for the consolidation of trial courts into a single set of courts or two sets of courts, one to hear major cases and one to hear minor cases.

A good deal of opposition has arisen to court unification. Many trial lawyers who are in court almost daily become accustomed to existing court organizations and, therefore, are opposed to change. Also, judges and other personnel associated with the courts are sometimes opposed to reform. Their opposition often grows out of fear — of being transferred to new courts, of having to learn new procedures, or of having to decide cases outside their area of specialization. The court unification movement, then, has not been as successful as many would like. On the other hand, proponents of court reform have secured victories in some states.

STATE COURT ORGANIZATION

Some states have moved in the direction of a unified court system, whereas others still operate with a bewildering complex of courts with overlapping jurisdiction. The state courts may be divided into four general categories or levels: trial courts of limited jurisdiction, trial courts of general jurisdiction, intermediate appellate courts, and courts of last resort.

Trial Courts of Limited Jurisdiction

Trial courts of limited jurisdiction handle the bulk of litigation in the United States each year and constitute about 90 percent of all courts. They have a variety of names: justice of the peace courts, magistrate courts, municipal courts, city courts, county courts, juvenile courts, domestic relations courts, and metropolitan courts, to name the more common ones.

The jurisdiction of these courts is limited to minor cases. In criminal matters, for example, state courts deal with three levels of violations: infractions (the least serious), misdemeanors (more serious), and felonies (the most serious). Trial courts of limited jurisdiction handle infractions and misdemeanors. They may impose only limited fines (usually no more than $1,000) and jail sentences (generally no more than one year). In civil cases these courts are usually limited to disputes under a certain amount, such as $500. In addition, these types of courts are often limited to certain kinds of matters: traffic violations, domestic relations, or cases involving juveniles, for example.

Another difference from trial courts of general jurisdiction is that in many instances these limited courts are not courts of record. Since their proceedings are not recorded, appeals of their decisions usually go to a trial court of general jurisdiction for what is known as a trial "de novo" (new trial). Yet another distinguishing characteristic of trial courts of limited jurisdiction is that the presiding judges of such courts are often not required to have any formal legal training.

Many of these courts suffer from a lack of resources. Often, they have no permanent courtroom, meeting instead in grocery stores, restaurants, or private homes. Clerks are frequently not available to keep adequate records. The results are informal proceedings and the processing of cases on a mass basis. Full-fledged trials are rare and cases are disposed of quickly.

Finally, trial courts of limited jurisdiction are used in some states to handle preliminary matters in felony criminal cases. They often hold arraignments, set bail, appoint attorneys for indigent defendants, and conduct preliminary examinations. The case is then transferred to a trial court of general jurisdiction for such matters as hearing pleas, holding trials, and sentencing.

Trial Courts of General Jurisdiction

Most states have one set of major trial courts that handle the more serious criminal and civil cases. In addition, in many states, special categories — such as juvenile criminal offenses, domestic relations cases, and probate cases — are under the jurisdiction of the general trial courts.

Attorney Edward Clancy, left, argues his case before his state's "court of last resort," the New Hampshire State Supreme Court.

Washington State's Supreme Court, like other state courts of last resort, follows procedures similar to those of the U.S. Supreme Court. Here, defense attorney Roger Hunko makes closing arguments in the penalty phase of a murder trial.

In most states these courts also have an appellate function. They hear appeals in certain types of cases that originate in trial courts of limited jurisdiction. These appeals are often heard in a trial de novo or tried again in the court of general jurisdiction.

General trial courts are usually divided into judicial districts or circuits. Although the practice varies by state, the general rule is to use existing political boundaries, such as a county or a group of counties, in establishing the district or circuit. In rural areas the judge may ride circuit and hold court in different parts of the territory according to a fixed schedule. In urban areas, however, judges hold court in a prescribed place throughout the year. In larger counties the group of judges may be divided into specializations. Some may hear only civil cases; others try criminal cases exclusively.

The courts at this level have a variety of names. The most common are district, circuit, and superior. The judges at this level are required by law in all states to have law degrees. These courts also maintain clerical help because they are courts of record.

Intermediate Appellate Courts

The intermediate appellate courts are relative newcomers to the state judicial scene. Only 13 such courts existed in 1911, whereas 39 states had created them by 1995. Their basic purpose is to relieve the workload of the state's highest court.

In most instances these courts are called courts of appeals, although other names are occasionally used. Most states have one court of appeals with statewide jurisdiction. The size of intermediate courts varies from state to state. The court of appeals in Alaska, for example, has only three judges. At the other extreme, Texas has 80 courts of appeals judges. In some states the intermediate appeals courts sit en banc, whereas in other states they sit in permanent or rotating panels.

Courts of Last Resort

Every state has a court of last resort. The states of Oklahoma and Texas have two highest courts. Both states have a supreme court with jurisdiction limited to appeals in civil cases and a court of criminal appeals for criminal cases. Most states call their highest courts supreme courts; other designations are the court of appeals (Maryland and New York), the supreme judicial court (Maine and Massachusetts), and the supreme court of appeals (West Virginia). The courts of last resort range in size from three to nine judges (or justices in some states). They typically sit en banc and usually, although not necessarily, convene in the state capital.

The highest courts have jurisdiction in matters pertaining to state law and are, of course, the final arbiters in such matters. In states that have intermediate appellate courts, the Supreme

New York and Maryland call their highest courts the "court of appeals." Pictured left to right are New York State Court of Appeals Judge George Bundy Smith, Chief Judge Judith S. Kaye, and Judge Howard A. Levine, as they listen to arguments in a death penalty case.

Court's cases come primarily from these mid-level courts. In this situation the high court typically is allowed to exercise discretion in deciding which cases to review. Thus, it is likely to devote more time to cases that deal with the important policy issues of the state. When there is no intermediate court of appeals, cases generally go to the state's highest court on a mandatory review basis.

In most instances, then, the state courts of last resort resemble the U.S. Supreme Court in that they have a good deal of discretion in determining which cases will occupy their atten-

tion. Most state supreme courts also follow procedures similar to those of the U.S. Supreme Court. That is, when a case is accepted for review the opposing parties file written briefs and later present oral arguments. Then, upon reaching a decision, the judges issue written opinions explaining that decision.

Juvenile Courts

Americans are increasingly concerned about the handling of cases involving juveniles, and states have responded to the problem in a variety of ways. Some have established a statewide network of courts specifically to handle matters involving juveniles. Two states — Rhode Island and South Carolina — have family courts, which handle domestic relations matters as well as those involving juveniles.

The most common approach is to give one or more of the state's limited or general trial courts jurisdiction to handle situations involving juveniles. In Alabama, for example, the circuit courts (trial courts of general jurisdiction) have jurisdiction over juvenile matters. In Kentucky, however, exclusive juvenile jurisdiction is lodged in trial courts of limited jurisdiction — the district courts.

Finally, some states apportion juvenile jurisdiction among more than one court. The state of Colorado has a juvenile court for the city of Denver and has given jurisdiction over juveniles to district courts (general trial courts) in the other areas of the state.

Also, some variation exists among the states as to when jurisdiction belongs to an adult court. States set a standard age at which defendants are tried in an adult court. In addition, many states require that more youthful offenders be tried in an adult court if special circumstances are present. In Illinois, for instance, the standard age at which juvenile jurisdiction transfers to adult courts is 17. The age limit drops to 15, however, for first-degree murder, aggravated criminal sexual assault, armed robbery, robbery with a firearm, and unlawful use of weapons on school grounds.

ADMINISTRATIVE AND STAFF SUPPORT IN THE STATE JUDICIARY

The daily operation of the federal courts requires the efforts of many individuals and organizations. This is no less true for the state court systems.

Magistrates

State magistrates, who may also be known in some states as commissioners or referees, are often used to perform some of the work in the early stages of civil and criminal case processing. In this way they are similar to U.S. magistrate judges. In some jurisdictions they hold bond hearings and conduct preliminary investigations in criminal cases. They are also authorized in some states to make decisions in minor cases.

Law Clerks

In the state courts, law clerks are likely to be found, if at all, in the intermediate appellate courts and courts of last resort. Most state trial courts do not utilize law clerks, and they are practically unheard of in local trial courts of limited jurisdiction. As at the national level, some law clerks serve individual judges while others serve an entire court as a staff attorney.

State courts handle millions of cases a year, at times in facilities like the Berkeley County Courthouse in Martinsburg, West Virginia, which some call "historic" or "charming" and others describe as "inadequate."

Administrative Office of the Courts

Every state now has an administrative office of courts or a similarly titled agency that performs a variety of administrative tasks for that state's court system. Among the tasks more commonly associated with administrative offices are budget preparation, data processing, facility management, judicial education, public information, research, and personnel management. Juvenile and adult probation are the responsibility of administrative offices in a few states, as is alternative dispute resolution.

Court Clerks and Court Administrators

The clerk of the court has traditionally handled the day-to-day routines of the court. This includes making courtroom arrangements, keeping records of case proceedings, preparing orders and judgments resulting from court actions, collecting court fines and fees, and disbursing judicial monies. In the majority of states these officials are elected and may be referred to by other titles.

The traditional clerks of court have been replaced in many areas by court administrators. In contrast to the court clerk, who traditionally managed the operations of a specific courtroom, the modern court administrator may assist a presiding judge in running the entire courthouse.

STATE COURT WORKLOAD

The lion's share of the nation's judicial business exists at the state, not the national, level. The fact that federal judges adjudicate several hundred thousand cases a year is impressive; the fact that state courts handle several million a year is overwhelming, even if the most important cases are handled at the federal level. While justice of the peace and magistrate courts at the state level handle relatively minor matters, some of the biggest judgments in civil cases are awarded by ordinary state trial court juries.

The National Center for State Courts has compiled figures on the caseloads of state courts of last resort and intermediate appellate courts in 1998. In all, some 261,159 mandatory cases and discretionary petitions were filed in the state appellate courts. Reliable data on cases filed in the state trial courts are harder to come by. Still, the center does an excellent job of tracking figures for states' trial courts. In 1998, 17,252,940 cases were filed in the general jurisdiction and limited jurisdiction courts. As with the federal courts, the vast majority of the cases are civil, although the criminal cases often receive the most publicity.   ⚖

JURISDICTION AND POLICY-MAKING BOUNDARIES

Beginning with the Supreme Court's decision in *Baker v. Carr* (1962), the Court has held in several cases that legislative districts should be of equal population size and that courts should see to it that this mandate is carried out. Here, Associate Justice Sarah Parker of the Supreme Court of North Carolina looks over a map during a court session dealing with redistricting, or reapportionment of legislative districts.

In setting the jurisdictions of courts, Congress and the U.S. Constitution — and their state counterparts — mandate the types of cases each court may hear. This chapter considers how Congress, in particular, can influence judicial behavior by redefining the types of cases judges may hear. It also discusses judicial self-restraint, examining 10 principles, derived from legal tradition and constitutional and statutory law, that govern a judge's decision about whether to review a case.

FEDERAL COURTS

The federal court system is divided into three separate levels: the trial courts, the appellate tribunals, and the U.S. Supreme Court.

U.S. District Courts

Congress has set forth the jurisdiction of the federal district courts. These tribunals have original jurisdiction in federal criminal and civil cases; that is, by law, the cases must be first heard in these courts, no matter who the parties are or how significant the issues.

Criminal Cases. These cases commence when the local U.S. attorneys have reason to believe that a violation of the U.S. Penal Code has occurred. After obtaining an indictment from a federal grand jury, the U.S. attorney files charges against the accused in the district court in which he or she serves. Criminal activity as defined by Congress covers a wide range of behavior, including interstate theft of an automobile, illegal importation of narcotics, assassination of a president, conspiracy to deprive persons of their civil rights, and even the killing of a migratory bird out of season.

After charges are filed against an accused, and if no plea bargain has been made, a trial is conducted by a U.S. district judge. In court the defendant enjoys all the privileges and immunities granted in the Bill of Rights (such as the right to a speedy and public trial) or by congressional legislation or Supreme Court rulings (for instance, a 12-person jury must render a unanimous verdict). Defendants may waive the right to a trial by a jury of their peers. A defendant who is found not guilty of the crime is set free and may never be tried again for the same offense (the Fifth Amendment's protection against double jeopardy). If the accused is found guilty, the district judge determines the appropriate sentence within a range set by Congress. The length of a sentence cannot be appealed so long as it is in the range prescribed. A verdict of not guilty may not be appealed by the government, but convicted defendants may appeal if they believe that the judge or jury made an improper legal determination.

Civil Cases. A majority of the district court caseload is civil in nature; that is, suits between private parties or between the U.S. government, acting in a nonprosecutorial capacity, and a private party. Civil cases that originate in the U.S. district courts may be placed in several categories. The first is litigation concerning the interpretation or application of the Constitution, acts of Congress, or U.S. treaties. Examples of cases in this category include the following: a petitioner claims that one of his or her federally protected civil rights has been violated, a litigant alleges that he or she is being harmed by a congressional statute that is unconstitutional, and a plaintiff argues that he or she is suffering injury from a treaty that is improperly affecting him. The key point is that a federal question must be raised in order for the U.S. trial courts to have jurisdiction.

Traditionally, some minimal dollar amounts had to be in controversy in some types of cases before the trial courts would hear them, but such amounts have been waived if the case falls into one of several general categories. For example, an alleged violation of a civil rights law, such as the Voting Rights Act of 1965, must be heard by the federal rather than the state judiciary. Other types of cases in this category are patent and copyright claims, passport and naturalization proceedings, admiralty and maritime disputes, and violations of the U.S. postal laws.

Another broad category of cases over which the U.S. trial courts exercise general original jurisdiction includes what are known as diversity of citizenship disputes. These are disputes between parties from different states or between an American citizen and a foreign country or citizen.

Federal district courts also have jurisdiction over petitions from convicted prisoners who contend that their incarceration (or perhaps their denial of parole) is in violation of their federally protected rights. In the vast majority of these cases prisoners ask for a writ of "habeas corpus" (Latin for "you should have the body"), an order issued by a judge to determine whether a person has been lawfully imprisoned or detained. The judge would demand that the prison authorities either justify the detention or release the petitioner. Prisoners convicted in a state court must argue that a federally protected right was violated — for example, the right to be represented by counsel at trial. Otherwise, the federal courts would have no jurisdiction. Federal prisoners have a somewhat wider range for their appeals since all their rights and options are within the scope of the U.S. Constitution.

Finally, the district courts have the authority to hear any other cases that Congress may validly prescribe by law.

U.S. Courts of Appeals

The U.S. appellate courts have no original jurisdiction whatsoever; every case or controversy that comes to one of these intermediate level panels has been first argued in some other forum.

Judges from the Appellate Division of the New York State Supreme Court in Rochester, New York, hear motion arguments. A dispute must be real and current before a court will agree to accept it for adjudication.

These tribunals, like the district courts, are the creations of Congress, and their structure and functions have varied considerably over time.

Basically, Congress has granted the circuit courts appellate jurisdiction over two general categories of cases. The first of these are ordinary civil and criminal appeals from the federal trial courts. In criminal cases the appellant is the defendant because the government is not free to appeal a verdict of not guilty. In civil cases the party that lost in the trial court is usually the appellant, but the winning party may appeal if it is not satisfied with the lower-court judgment. The second broad category of appellate jurisdiction includes appeals from certain federal administrative agencies and departments and also from independent regulatory commissions, such as the Securities and Exchange Commission and the National Labor Relations Board.

U.S. Supreme Court

The U.S. Supreme Court is the only federal court mentioned by name in the Constitution, which spells out the general contours of the High Court's jurisdiction. Although the Supreme Court is usually thought of as an appellate tribunal, it does have some general original jurisdiction. Probably the most important subject of such jurisdiction is a suit between two or more states.

The High Court shares original jurisdiction (with the U.S. district courts) in certain cases brought by or against foreign ambassadors or consuls, in cases between the United States and a state, and in cases commenced by a state against citizens of another state or another country. In situations such as these, where jurisdiction is shared, the courts are said to have concurrent jurisdiction. Cases over which the Supreme Court has original jurisdiction are often important, but they do not constitute a sizable proportion of the overall caseload. In recent years less than 1 percent of the High Court's docket consisted of cases heard on original jurisdiction.

The U.S. Constitution declares that the Supreme Court "shall have appellate Jurisdiction...under such Regulations as the Congress shall make." Over the years Congress has passed much legislation setting forth the "Regulations" determining which cases may appear before the nation's most august judicial body. Appeals may reach the Supreme Court through two main avenues. First, there may be appeals from all lower federal constitutional and territorial courts and also from most, but not all, federal legislative courts. Second, the Supreme Court may hear appeals from the highest court in a state — as long as there is a substantial federal question.

Most of the High Court's docket consists of cases in which it has agreed to issue a writ of certiorari — a discretionary action. Such a writ (which must be supported by at least four justices) is an order from the Supreme Court to a lower court demanding that it send up a complete record of a case so that the Supreme Court can review it. Historically, the Supreme Court has agreed to grant the petition for a writ of certiorari in only a tiny proportion of cases — usually less than 10 percent of the time, and in recent years the number has been closer to 1 percent.

Another method by which the Supreme Court exercises its appellate jurisdiction is certification. This procedure is followed when one of the appeals courts asks the Supreme Court for instructions regarding a question of law. The justices may choose to give the appellate judges binding instructions, or they may ask that the entire record be forwarded to the Supreme Court for review and final judgment.

JURISDICTION AND POLICY MAKING OF STATE COURTS

The jurisdictions of the 50 separate state court systems in the United States are established in virtually the same manner as those within the national court system. Each state has a constitution that sets forth the authority and decision-making powers of its trial and appellate judges. Likewise, each state legislature passes laws that further detail the specific powers and prerogatives of judges and the rights and obligations of those who bring suit in the state courts. Because no two state constitutions or legislative bodies are alike, the jurisdictions of individual state courts vary from one state to another.

State courts are extremely important in terms of policy making in the United States. Well over 99 percent of the judicial workload in the United States consists of state, not federal, cases, and 95 percent of all judges in the United States work at the state level. Moreover, the decisions of state jurists frequently have a great impact on public policy. For example, during the 1970s a number of suits were brought into federal court challenging the constitutionality of a state's spending vastly unequal sums on the education of its schoolchildren. (This occurred because poorer school districts could not raise the same amount of money as could wealthy school districts.) The litigants claimed that children in the poorer districts were victims of unlawful discrimination in violation of their equal protection rights under the U.S. Constitution. The Supreme Court said they were not, however, in a five-to-four decision in *San Antonio Independent School District v. Rodriguez* (1973). But the matter did not end there. Litigation was instituted in many states arguing that unequal educational opportunities were in violation of various clauses in the state constitutions. Since *Rodriguez* such suits have been brought 28 times in 24 states. In 14 of these cases, state supreme courts invalidated their state's method of financing education, thus requiring the reallocation of billions of dollars.

JURISDICTION AND LEGISLATIVE POLITICS

Some judges and judicial scholars argue that the U.S. Constitution and the respective state documents confer a certain inherent jurisdiction upon the judiciaries in some key areas, independent of the legislative will. Nevertheless, the jurisdictional boundaries of American courts are also a product of legislative judgments — determinations often influenced by politics.

Congress may advance a particular cause by giving courts the authority to hear cases in a public policy realm that previously had been forbidden territory for the judiciary. For example, when Congress passed the Civil Rights Act of 1968, it gave judges the authority to penalize individuals who interfere with "any person because of his race, color, religion or national origin and because he is or has been...traveling in...interstate commerce." Prior to 1968 the courts had no jurisdiction over incidents that stemmed from interference by one person with another's right to travel. Likewise, Congress may discourage a particular social movement by passing legislation to make it virtually impossible for its advocates to have any success in the courts.

The jurisdictions of state courts, like their federal counterparts, also are very much governed by — and the political product of — the will of the state legislatures.

JUDICIAL SELF-RESTRAINT

The activities that judges are forbidden to engage in, or at least discouraged from engaging in, deal not so much with jurisdiction as with justiciability — the question of whether judges in the system ought to hear or refrain from hearing certain types of disputes. Ten principles of judicial self-restraint, discussed below, serve to check and contain the power of American judges. These maxims originate from a variety of sources — the U.S. Constitution and state constitutions, acts of Congress and of state legislatures, and the common law. Some apply more to appellate courts than to trial courts; most apply to federal and state judicial systems.

A Definite Controversy Must Exist

The U.S. Constitution states that "the judicial Power shall extend to all Cases, in Law and Equity, arising under this Constitution, the Laws of the United States, and Treaties made...under their Authority" (Article III, Section 2). The key word here is cases. Since 1789 the federal courts have chosen to interpret the term in its most literal sense: There must be an actual controversy between legitimate adversaries who have met all the technical legal standards to institute a suit. The dispute must concern the protection of a meaningful, nontrivial right or the prevention or redress of a wrong that directly affects the parties to the suit. There are three corollaries to this general principle.

The first is that the federal courts do not render advisory opinions, rulings about situations that are hypothetical or that have not caused an actual clash between adversaries. A dispute must be real and current before a court will agree to accept it for adjudication.

A second corollary is that the parties to the suit must have proper standing. This notion deals with the matter of who may bring litigation to court. The person bringing suit must have suffered (or be immediately about to suffer) a direct and significant injury. As a general rule, a litigant cannot bring a claim on behalf of others (except for parents of minor children or in special types of suits called class actions). In addition, the alleged injury must be personalized and immediate — not part of some generalized complaint.

The third corollary is that courts ordinarily will not hear a case that has become moot — when the basic facts or the status of the parties have significantly changed between the time when the suit was first filed and when it comes before the judge(s). The death of a litigant or the fact that the litigants have ceased to be warring parties would render a case moot in most tribunals. However, sometimes judges may decide that it is necessary to hear a case, even though the status of the facts and parties would seem to have radically altered. Examples include cases where someone has challenged a state's refusal to permit an abortion or to permit the life-support system of a terminally ill person to be switched off. (In such cases, by the time the suit reaches an appellate court, the woman may already have given birth or the moribund person may have died.) In these cases judges have believed that the issues were so important that they needed to be addressed by the court. To declare such cases moot would, practically speaking, prevent them from ever being heard in time by an appellate body.

Although federal judges do not rule on abstract, hypothetical issues, many state courts are permitted to do so in some form or other. Federal legislative courts may give advisory opinions as well. Also, American judges are empowered to render declaratory judgments, which define the rights of various parties under a statute, a will, or a contract. The judgments do not entail any type of coercive relief. The federal courts were given the authority to act in this capacity in the Federal Declaratory Judgment Act of 1934, and about three-fourths of the states grant their courts this power. Although a difference exists between an abstract dispute that the federal courts

must avoid and a situation where a declaratory judgment is in order, in the real world the line between the two is often a difficult one for jurists to draw.

A Plea Must Be Specific

Another constraint upon the federal judiciary is that judges will hear no case on the merits unless the petitioner is first able to cite a specific part of the Constitution as the basis of the plea. For example, the First Amendment forbids government from making a law "respecting an establishment of religion." In 1989 the state of New York created a special school district solely for the benefit of the Satmar Hasids, a group of Hasidic Jews with East European roots that strongly resists assimilation into modern society. Most of the children attended parochial schools in the Village of Kiryas Joel, but these private schools weren't able to accommodate retarded and disabled students, and the Satmars claimed that such children within their community would be traumatized if forced to attend a public school. Responding to this situation, the state legislature created a special district encompassing a single school that served only handicapped children from the Hasidic Jewish community. This arrangement was challenged by the association representing New York state's school boards. In June 1994 the U.S. Supreme Court ruled that the creation of the one-school district effectively delegated political power to the

Circuit courts have appellate jurisdiction over civil appeals from the federal trial courts, such as a 2000 case where the 4th U.S. Circuit Court of Appeals was asked to overturn a federal judge's ruling that the mining industry claimed would end mining in the Appalachian Mountains (shown above). These courts also can hear appeals from certain federal administrative agencies. The two juvenile Mexican spotted owls, left, however, appear unaware that a suit by an environmental group, the Audubon Society, involves their species's habitats.

Congress has said that federal district courts have jurisdiction in federal civil and criminal cases. In this photo, Justice Department lead attorney David Boies, left, and Connecticut Attorney General Richard Blumenthal, right, discuss the Microsoft Windows 98 case with the media.

orthodox Jewish group and therefore violated the First Amendment's ban on governmental "establishment of religion." Whether or not everyone agrees that the New York law was constitutional, few, if any, would doubt that the school board association met the specific criteria for securing judicial review: The Constitution clearly forbids the government from delegating political power to a specific religious entity. The government here readily acknowledged that it had passed a law for the unique benefit of a singular religious community.

However, if one went into court and contended that a particular law or official action "violated the spirit of the Bill of Rights" or "offended the values of the Founders," a judge surely would dismiss the proceeding. For if judges were free to give concrete, substantive meaning to vague generalities such as these, there would be little check on what they could do. In the real world this principle is not as simple and clear-cut as it sounds, because the Constitution contains many clauses that are open to a wide variety of interpretations, giving federal judges sufficient room to maneuver and make policy.

Beneficiaries May Not Sue

A third aspect of judicial self-restraint is that a petitioner who has been the beneficiary of a law or an official action may not subsequently challenge that law. For example, suppose that a farmer has long been a member of a program under which he agreed to take part of his land out of production and periodically was paid a subsidy by the federal government. After years as a participant, the farmer learns that a neighbor is also drawing regular payments for letting all of his farmland lie fallow. The idea that the neighbor is getting something for nothing offends the farmer, and he questions the program's constitutionality. The farmer challenges the legality of the program in the local federal district court. As soon as it is brought to the judge's attention that the farmer had himself been a member of the program and had gained financially from it, the suit is dismissed: One may not benefit from a particular governmental endeavor or official action and subsequently attack it in court.

Appellate Courts Rule on Legal — Not Factual — Questions

A working proposition of state and federal appellate court practice is that these courts will generally not hear cases if the grounds for appeal are that the trial judge or jury wrongly amassed and identified the basic factual elements of the case. It is not that trial judges and juries always do a perfect job of making factual determinations. Rather, there is the belief that they are closer to the actual parties and physical evidence of the case, and, therefore, they will do a much better job of making factual assessments than would an appellate body reading a transcript of the case some months or years after the trial. However, legal matters — which laws to apply to the facts of a case or how to assess the facts in light of the prevailing law — are appropriate for appellate review.

The Supreme Court Is Not Bound (Technically) by Precedents

If the High Court is free to overturn or circumvent past and supposedly controlling precedents when it decides a case, this might appear to be an argument for judicial activism — not restraint. However, this practice is one of the principles of self-restraint. If the Supreme Court were inescapably bound by the dictates of its prior rulings, it would have very little flexibility. By occasionally allowing itself the freedom to overrule a past decision or to ignore a precedent that would seem to be controlling, the Supreme Court establishes a corner of safety to which it can retreat if need be. When wisdom dictates that the Court change direction or at least keep an open mind, this principle of self-restraint is put to use.

Other Remedies Must Be Exhausted

Another principle of self-restraint often frustrates the anxious litigant but is essential to the orderly administration of justice: Courts in the United States will not accept a case until all other remedies, legal and administrative, have been exhausted. In its simplest form this doctrine means that one must work up the ladder with one's legal petitions. Federal cases must first be heard by the U.S. trial courts, then reviewed by one of the appellate tribunals, and finally heard by the U.S. Supreme Court. This orderly procedure of events must occur despite the importance of the case or of the petitioners who filed it. In certain circumstances, however, the appellate process can be shortened.

Exhaustion of remedies refers to possible administrative relief as well as to adherence to the principle of a three-tiered judicial hierarchy. Such relief might be in the form of an appeal to an administrative officer, a hearing before a board or committee, or formal consideration of a matter by a legislative body.

Courts Do Not Decide "Political Questions"

To U.S. judges, the executive and the legislative branches of government are political in that they are elected by the people for the purpose of making public policy. The judiciary, in contrast, was not designed by the Founders to be an instrument manifesting the popular will and is therefore not political. According to this line of reasoning, then, a political question is one that ought properly to be resolved by one of the other two branches of government.

For example, when the state of Oregon gave its citizens the right to vote on popular statewide referendums and initiatives around 1900, the Pacific States Telephone and Telegraph Company objected. (The company feared that voters would bypass the more business-oriented legislature and pass laws restricting its rates and profits.) The company claimed that Article IV, Section 4, of the Constitution guarantees to each state "a Republican Form of Government" — a term that supposedly means that laws are to be made only by the elected representatives of the people, not by the citizens directly. The High Court refused to rule on the merits of the case, declaring the issue to be a political question. The Court reasoned that since Article IV primarily prescribes the duties of Congress, it follows that the Founders wanted Congress — not the courts — to oversee the forms of government in the several states.

In recent decades an important political versus nonpolitical dispute has concerned the matter of reapportionment of legislative districts. Prior to 1962, a majority on the Supreme Court refused to rule on the constitutionality of legislative districts with unequal populations, saying that such matters were "nonjusticiable" and that the Court dared not enter what Justice Felix Frankfurter called "the political thicket." According to traditional Supreme Court thinking,

the Founders wanted legislatures to redistrict themselves — perhaps with input from the electorate. However, with the Supreme Court's decision in *Baker v. Carr* (1962), the majority reversed that thinking. Since then the Court has held in scores of cases that the equal-protection clause of the Fourteenth Amendment requires legislative districts to be of equal population size and, furthermore, that the courts should see to it that this mandate is carried out.

The Burden of Proof Is on the Petitioner

The nation's jurists generally agree that an individual who would challenge the constitutionality of a statute bears the burden of proof. Thus, if someone were to attack a particular statute, he or she would have to do more than demonstrate that it was "questionable or of doubtful constitutionality"; the petitioner would have to persuade the court that the evidence against the law was clear-cut and overwhelming.

The only exception to this burden of proof principle is in the realm of civil rights and liberties. Some jurists who are strong civil libertarians have long contended that when government attempts to restrict basic human freedoms the burden of proof should shift to the government. And in several specific areas of civil rights jurisprudence that philosophy now prevails. For example, the U.S.

Supreme Court has ruled in a variety of cases that laws that treat persons differently according to their race or gender are automatically subject to "special scrutiny." This means that the burden of proof shifts to the government to demonstrate a compelling or overriding need to differentiate persons according to their ethnic origins or sex. For instance, the government has long argued (successfully) that some major restrictions can be placed on women in the armed forces that prevent them from being assigned to full combat duty.

Laws Are Overturned on the Narrowest Grounds Only

Sometimes during a trial a judge clearly sees that the strictures of the Constitution have been offended by a legislative or executive act. Even here, however, a jurist may proceed with caution. First, a judge may have the option of invalidating an official action on what is called statutory, instead of constitutional, grounds. Statutory invalidation means that a judge overturns an official's action because the official acted beyond the authority delegated to him or her by the law. Such a ruling has the function of saving the law itself while still nullifying the official's misdeed. Second, judges may, if possible, invalidate only that portion of a law they find constitutionally defective instead of overturning the entire statute.

No Rulings Are Made on the "Wisdom" of Legislation

If followed strictly, this principle means that the only basis for declaring a law or an official action unconstitutional is that it literally violates the Constitution. Statutes do not offend the Constitution merely because they are unfair, are fiscally wasteful, or constitute bad public policy. If taken truly to heart, this means that judges and justices are not free to invoke their own personal notions of right and wrong or of good and bad public policy when they examine the constitutionality of legislation.

Another spinoff of this principle is that a law may be passed that all agree is good and wise but that is nevertheless unconstitutional; conversely, a statute may legalize the commission of an official deed that all know to be bad and dangerous but that still does not offend the Constitution.

The principle of not ruling on the "wisdom" of a law is difficult to follow in the real world. This is so because the Constitution, a rather brief document, is silent on many areas of public life and contains a number of phrases and admonitions that are open to a variety of interpretations. For instance, the Constitution says that Congress may regulate interstate commerce. But what exactly is commerce, and how extensive does it have to be before it is of an "interstate" character? As human beings, judges have differed in the way they have responded to this question. The Constitution guarantees a person accused of a crime the right to a defense attorney. But does this right continue if one appeals a guilty verdict and, if so, for how many appeals? Strict constructionists and loose constructionists have responded differently to these queries.

In all, despite the inevitable intrusion of judges' personal values into their interpretation of many portions of the Constitution, virtually every jurist subscribes to the general principle that laws can be invalidated only if they offend the Constitution — not the personal preferences of the judges.   ⚖

LAWYERS, LITIGANTS, AND INTEREST GROUPS IN THE JUDICIAL PROCESS

New lawyers take their oaths in Topeka, Kansas, to practice in the Kansas state court and in the Federal court in the district of Kansas. According to recent estimates, the United States has more than 950,000 lawyers.

This chapter focuses on three crucial actors in the judicial process: lawyers, litigants, and interest groups. Judges in the United States make decisions only in the context of cases that are brought to the courts by individuals or groups who have some sort of disagreement or dispute with each other. These adversaries, commonly called litigants, sometimes argue their own cases in such minor forums as small claims courts, but they are almost always represented by lawyers in the more important judicial arenas. Following an examination of the legal profession, the chapter discusses the role of individual litigants and interest groups in the judicial process.

LAWYERS AND THE LEGAL PROFESSION

The training of attorneys and the practice of law have evolved over time in the United States. Today American lawyers practice in a variety of settings and circumstances.

Development of the Legal Profession

During the colonial period in America (1607-1776), there were no law schools to train those interested in the legal profession. Some young men went to England for their education and attended the Inns of Court. The Inns were not formal law schools, but were part of the English legal culture and allowed students to become familiar with English law.

Those who aspired to the law during this period generally performed a clerkship or apprenticeship with an established lawyer.

After the American Revolution (1775-83), the number of lawyers increased rapidly, because neither legal education nor admission to the bar was very strict. The apprenticeship method continued to be the most popular way to receive legal training, but law schools began to come into existence. The first law schools grew out of law offices that specialized in training clerks or apprentices. The earliest such school was the Litchfield School in Connecticut, founded in 1784. This school, which taught by the lecture method, placed primary emphasis on commercial law. Eventually, a few colleges began to teach law as part of their general curriculum, and in 1817 an independent law school was established at Harvard University.

During the second half of the 19th century, the number of law schools increased dramatically, from 15 schools in 1850 to 102 in 1900. The law schools of that time and those of today have two major differences. First, law schools then did not usually require any previous college work. Second, in 1850 the standard law school curriculum could be completed in one year. Later in the 1800s many law schools instituted two-year programs.

In 1870 major changes began at Harvard that were to have a lasting impact on legal training. Harvard instituted stiffer entrance requirements; a student who did not have a college degree was required to pass an entrance test. The law school course was increased to two years in 1871 and to three years in 1876. Also, students were required to pass first-year final examinations before proceeding to the second-year courses.

The most lasting change, however, was the introduction of the case method of teaching. This method replaced lectures and textbooks with casebooks. The casebooks (collections of actual case reports) were designed to explain the principles of law, what they meant, and how they developed. Teachers then used the Socratic method to guide the students to a discovery of legal concepts found in the cases. Other schools eventually adopted the Harvard approach, and the case method remains the accepted method of teaching in many law schools today.

As the demand for lawyers increased during the late 1800s, there was a corresponding acceleration in the creation of new law schools. Opening a law school was not expensive, and a number of night schools, using lawyers and judges as part-time faculty members, sprang into existence. Standards were often lax and the curriculum tended to emphasize local practice. These schools' major contribution lay in making training more readily available to poor, immigrant, and working-class students.

In the 20th century, the number of people wanting to study law increased dramatically. By the 1960s the number of applicants to law schools had grown so large that nearly all schools became more selective. At the same time, in response to social pressure and litigation, many law schools began actively recruiting female and minority applicants.

Also by the 1960s, the curriculum in some law schools had been expanded to include social concerns such as civil rights law and law-and-poverty issues. International law courses also became available.

A more recent trend in law schools is an emphasis on the use of computers for everything from registration to classroom instruction to accessing court forms to student services. Also noteworthy is that more and more law schools are offering courses or special programs in intellectual property law, a field of specialization that has grown considerably in recent years. Finally, the increasing use of advertising by lawyers has had a profound impact on the legal profession. On television stations across the country one can now see lawyers making appeals to attract new clients. Furthermore, legal clinics, established to handle the business generated by the increased use of advertising, have spread rapidly.

Growth and Stratification

The number of lawyers in the United States has increased steadily over the past half century and is currently estimated at more than 950,000. Where do all the attorneys in the United States find work?

The Law School Admission Council provides some answers in *The Official Guide to U.S. Law Schools*, 2001 Edition. Almost three-fourths (72.9 percent) of America's lawyers are in private practice, some in small, one-person offices and some in much larger law firms. About 8.2 percent of the legal profession's members work for government agencies, roughly 9.5 percent work for private industries and associations as lawyers or managers, about 1.1 percent work for legal aid associations or as public defenders, representing those who cannot afford to pay a lawyer, and 1 percent are in legal education. Some 5 percent of the nation's lawyers are retired or inactive.

America's lawyers apply their professional training in a variety of settings. Some environments are more profitable and prestigious than others. This situation has led to what is known as professional stratification.

One of the major factors influencing the prestige level is the type of legal specialty and the type of clientele served. Lawyers with specialties who serve big business and large institutions occupy the top hemisphere; those who represent individual interests are in the bottom hemisphere.

At the top of the prestige ladder are the large national law firms. Attorneys in these firms have traditionally been known less for court appearances than for the counseling they provide their clients. The clients must be able to pay for this high-powered legal tal-

The large national law firms employ associates, librarians, and paralegals to help partners with a myriad of tasks, such as research.

ent, and thus they tend to be major corporations rather than individuals. However, many of these large national firms often provide "pro bono" (Latin for "the public good," or free) legal services to further civil rights, civil liberties, consumer interests, and environmental causes.

The large national firms consist of partners and associates. Partners own the law firm and are paid a share of the firm's profits. The associates are paid salaries and in essence work for the partners. These large firms compete for the best graduates from the nation's law schools. The most prestigious firms have 250 or more lawyers and also employ hundreds of other people as paralegals (nonlawyers who are specially trained to handle many of the routine aspects of legal work), administrators, librarians, and secretaries.

A notch below those working in the large national firms are those employed as attorneys by large corporations. Many corporations use national law firms as outside counsel. Increasingly, however, corporations are hiring their own salaried attorneys as in-house counsel. The legal staff of some corporations rivals those of private firms in size. Further, these corporations compete with the major law firms for the best law school graduates.

Instead of representing the corporation in court (a task usually handled by outside counsel when necessary), the legal division handles the multitude of legal problems faced by the modern corporation. For example, the legal division monitors the company's personnel practices to ensure compliance with federal and state regulations concerning hiring and removal procedures. The corporation's attorneys may advise the board of directors about such things as contractual agreements, mergers, stock sales, and other business practices. The company lawyers may also help educate other employees about the laws that apply to their specific jobs and make sure that they are in compliance with them. The legal division of a large company also serves as a liaison with outside counsel.

Most of the nation's lawyers work in a lower hemisphere of the legal profession in terms of prestige and do not command the high salaries associated with large national law firms and major corporations. However, they are engaged in a wider range of activities and are much more likely to be found, day in and day out, in the courtrooms of the United States. These are the attorneys who represent clients in personal injury suits, who prosecute and defend persons accused of crimes, who represent husbands and wives in divorce proceedings, who help people conduct real estate transactions, and who help people prepare wills, to name just a few activities.

Attorneys who work for the government are generally included in the lower hemisphere. Some, such as the U.S. attorney general and the solicitor general of the United States, occupy quite prestigious positions, but many toil in rather obscure and poorly paid positions. A number of attorneys opt for careers as judges at the federal or state level.

Another distinction in terms of specialization in the legal profession is that between plaintiffs and defense attorneys. The former group initiates lawsuits, whereas the latter group defends those accused of wrongdoing in civil and criminal cases.

Government Attorneys in the Judicial Process

Government attorneys work at all levels of the judicial process, from trial courts to the highest state and federal appellate courts.

Federal Prosecutors. Each federal judicial district has one U.S. attorney and one or more assistant U.S. attorneys. They are responsible for prosecuting defendants in criminal cases in the federal district courts and for defending the United States when it is sued in a federal trial court.

U.S. attorneys are appointed by the president and confirmed by the Senate. Nominees must reside in the district to which they are appointed and must be lawyers. They serve a formal term of four years but can be reappointed indefinitely or removed at the president's discretion. The assis-

tant U.S. attorneys are formally appointed by the U.S. attorney general, although in practice they are chosen by the U.S. attorney for the district, who forwards the selection to the attorney general for ratification. Assistant U.S. attorneys may be fired by the attorney general.

In their role as prosecutors, U.S. attorneys have considerable discretion in deciding which criminal cases to prosecute. They also have the authority to determine which civil cases to try to settle out of court and which ones to take to trial. U.S. attorneys, therefore, are in a very good position to influence the federal district court's docket. Also, because they engage in more litigation in the district courts than anyone else, the U.S. attorneys and their staffs are vital participants in policy making in the federal trial courts.

Prosecutors at the State Level. Those who prosecute persons accused of violating state criminal statutes are commonly known as district attorneys. In most states they are elected county officials; however, in a few states they are appointed. The district attorney's office usually employs a number of assistants who do most of the actual trial work. Most of these assistant district attorneys are recent graduates of law school, who gain valuable trial experience in these positions. Many later enter private practice, often as criminal defense attorneys. Others will seek to become district attorneys or judges after a few years.

The district attorney's office has a great deal of discretion in the handling of cases. Given budget and personnel constraints, not all cases can be afforded the same amount of time and attention. Therefore, some cases are dismissed, others are not prosecuted, and still others are prosecuted vigorously in court. Most cases, however, are subject to plea bargaining. This means that the district attorney's office agrees to accept the defendant's plea of guilty to a reduced charge or to drop some charges against the defendant in exchange for pleas of guilty to others.

Public Defenders. Often the person charged with violating a state or federal criminal statute is unable to pay for the services of a defense attorney. In some areas a government official known as a public defender bears the responsibility for representing indigent defendants. Thus, the public defender is a counterpart of the prosecutor. Unlike the district attorney, however, the public defender is usually appointed rather than elected.

In some parts of the country there are statewide public defender systems; in other regions the public defender is a local official, usually associated with a county government. Like the district attorney, the public defender employs assistants and investigative personnel.

In some areas, if a person charged with violating a state or federal criminal statute is unable to pay for the services of a defense attorney — as happened with the defendant above, center, facing the judge — a government official known as the public defender is responsible for representing the defendant.

Other Government Lawyers. At both the state and federal levels, some government attorneys are better known for their work in appellate courts than in trial courts. For example, each state has an attorney general who supervises a staff of attorneys who are charged with the responsibility of handling the legal affairs of the state. At the federal level the Department of Justice has similar responsibilities on behalf of the United States.

The U.S. Department of Justice. Although the Justice Department is an agency of the executive branch of the government, it has a natural association with the judicial branch. Many of the cases heard in the federal courts involve the national government in one capacity or another. Sometimes the government is sued; in other instances the government initiates the lawsuit. In either case, an attorney must represent the government. Most of the litigation involving the federal government is handled by the Justice Department, although a number of other government agencies have attorneys on their payrolls.

The Justice Department's Office of the Solicitor General is extremely important in cases argued before the Supreme Court. The department also has several legal divisions, each with a staff of specialized lawyers and headed by an assistant attorney general. The legal divisions supervise the handling of litigation by the U.S. attorneys, take cases to the courts of appeals, and aid the solicitor general's office in cases argued before the Supreme Court.

U.S. Solicitor General. The solicitor general of the United States, the third-ranking official in the Justice Department, is assisted by five deputies and about 20 assistant solicitors general. The solicitor general's primary function is to decide, on behalf of the United States, which cases will and will not be presented to the Supreme Court for review. Whenever an executive branch department or agency loses a case in one of the courts of appeals and wishes a Supreme Court review, that department or agency will request that the Justice Department seek certiorari. The solicitor general will determine whether to appeal the lower court decision.

Many factors must be taken into account when making such a decision. Perhaps the most important consideration is that the Supreme Court is limited in the number of cases it can hear in a given term. Thus, the solicitor general must determine whether a particular case deserves extensive consideration by the Court. In addition to deciding whether to seek Supreme Court review, the solicitor general personally argues most of the government's cases heard by the High Court.

State Attorneys General. Each state has an attorney general who serves as its chief legal official. In most states this official is elected on a partisan statewide ballot. The attorney general oversees a staff of attorneys who primarily handle the civil cases involving the state. Although the prosecution of criminal defendants is generally handled by the local district attorneys, the attorney general's office often plays an important role in investigating statewide criminal activities. Thus, the attorney general and his or her staff may work closely with the local district attorney in preparing a case against a particular defendant.

The state attorneys general also issue advisory opinions to state and local agencies. Often, these opinions interpret an aspect of state law not yet ruled on by the courts. Although an advisory opinion might eventually be overruled in a case brought before the courts, the attorney general's opinion is important in determining the behavior of state and local agencies.

Private Lawyers in the Judicial Process

In criminal cases in the United States the defendant has a constitutional right to be represented by an attorney. Some jurisdictions have established public defender's offices to represent indigent defendants. In other areas, some method exists of assigning a private attorney to represent a defendant who cannot afford to hire one. Those defendants who can afford to hire their own lawyers will do so.

In civil cases neither the plaintiff nor the defendant is constitutionally entitled to the services of an attorney. However, in the civil arena the legal issues are often so complex as to demand the services of an attorney. Various forms of legal assistance are usually available to those who need help.

Assigned Defense Counsel. When a private lawyer must be appointed to represent an indigent defendant, the assignment usually is made by an individual judge on an ad hoc basis. Local bar associations or lawyers themselves often provide the courts with a list of attorneys who are willing to provide such services.

Private Defense Counsel. Some attorneys in private practice specialize in criminal defense work. Although the lives of criminal defense attorneys may be depicted as glamorous on television and in movies, the average real-life criminal defense lawyer works long hours for low pay and low prestige.

The Courtroom Workgroup

Rather than functioning as an occasional gathering of strangers who resolve a particular conflict and then go their separate ways, lawyers and judges who work in a criminal court room become part of a workgroup.

The most visible members of the courtroom workgroup — judges, prosecutors, and defense attorneys — are associated with specific functions: Prosecutors push for convictions of those accused of criminal offenses against the government, defense attorneys seek acquittals for their clients, and judges serve as neutral arbiters to guarantee a fair trial. Despite their different roles, members of the courtroom workgroup share certain values and goals and are not the fierce adversaries that many people imagine. Cooperation among judges, prosecutors, and defense attorneys is the norm.

The most important goal of the courtroom workgroup is to handle cases expeditiously. Judges and prosecutors are interested in disposing of cases quickly to present a picture of accomplishment and efficiency. Because private defense attorneys need to handle a large volume of cases to survive financially, resolving cases quickly works to their advantage. And public defenders seek quick dispositions simply because they lack adequate resources to handle their caseloads.

A second important goal of the courtroom workgroup is to maintain group cohesion. Conflict among the members makes work more difficult and interferes with the expeditious handling of cases.

Finally, the courtroom workgroup is interested in reducing or controlling uncertainty. In practice this means that all members of the workgroup strive to avoid trials. Trials, especially jury trials, produce a great deal of uncertainty given that they require substantial investments of time and effort without any reasonable guarantee of a desirable outcome.

To attain these goals, workgroup members employ several techniques. Although unilateral decisions and adversarial proceedings occur, negotiation is the most commonly used technique in criminal courtrooms. The members negotiate over a variety of issues — continuances (delays in the court proceedings), hearing dates, and exchange of information, for example. Plea bargaining, however, is the most critical tool of negotiation.

Legal Services for the Poor

Although criminal defendants are constitutionally entitled to be represented by a lawyer, those who are defendants in a civil case or who wish to initiate a civil case do not have the right to representation. Therefore, those who do not have the funds to hire a lawyer may find it difficult to obtain justice.

To deal with this problem, legal aid services are now found in many areas. Legal aid societies were established in New York and Chicago as early as the late 1880s, and many other major cities followed suit in the 20th century. Although some legal aid societies are sponsored by bar associations, most are supported by private contributions. Legal aid bureaus also are associated with charitable organizations in some areas, and many law schools operate legal aid clinics to provide both legal assistance for the poor and valuable training for law students. In addition, many lawyers provide legal services "pro bono publico" (Latin for "for the public good") because they see it as a professional obligation.

LITIGANTS

In some cases taken before the courts, the litigants are individuals, whereas in other cases one or more of the litigants may be a government agency, a corporation, a union, an interest group, or a university.

What motivates a person or group to take a grievance to court? In criminal cases the answer to this question is relatively simple. A state or federal criminal statute has allegedly been violated, and the government prosecutes the party charged with violating the statute. In civil cases the answer is not quite so easy. Although some persons readily take their grievances to court, many others avoid this route because of the time and expense involved.

Political scientist Phillip Cooper points out that judges are called upon to resolve two kinds of disputes: private law cases and public law controversies. Private law disputes are those in which one private citizen or organization sues another. In public law controversies, a citizen or organization contends that a government agency or official has violated a right established by a constitution or statute. In *Hard Judicial Choices*, Cooper writes that "legal actions, whether public law or private law

contests, may either be policy oriented or compensatory."

A classic example of private, or ordinary, compensation-oriented litigation is when a person injured in an automobile accident sues the driver of the other car in an effort to win monetary damages as compensation for medical expenses incurred. This type of litigation is personal and is not aimed at changing governmental or business policies.

Some private law cases, however, are policy oriented or political in nature. Personal injury suits and product liability suits may appear on the surface to be simply compensatory in nature but may also be used to change the manufacturing or business practices of the private firms being sued.

A case litigated in North Carolina provides a good example. The case began in 1993 after a five-year-old girl got stuck on the drain of a wading pool after another child had removed the drain cover. Such a powerful suction was created that, before she could be rescued, the drain had sucked out most of her large and small intestines. As a result, the girl will have to spend about 11 hours per day attached to intravenous feeding tubes for the rest of her life. In 1997 a jury awarded the girl's family $25 million in compensatory damages and, before the jury was to have considered punitive damages, the drain manufacturer and two other defendants settled the case for $30.9 million. The plaintiff's attorney said that the lawsuit revealed similar incidents in other areas of the country and presented a stark example of something industry insiders knew but others did not. Not only did the family win its lawsuit, but the North Carolina legislature also passed a law requiring multiple drains to prevent such injuries in the future.

Most political or policy-oriented lawsuits, however, are public law controversies. That is, they are suits brought against the government primarily to stop allegedly illegal policies or practices. They may also seek damages or some other specific form of relief. A case decided by the U.S. Supreme Court, *Lucas v. South Carolina Coastal Council*, provides a good example. South Carolina's Beachfront Management Act forbade David H. Lucas from building single-family houses on two beachfront lots he owned. A South Carolina trial court ruled that Lucas was entitled to be compensated for his loss. The South Carolina Supreme Court reversed the trial court decision, however, and Lucas appealed to the U.S. Supreme Court. The High Court ruled in Lucas's favor, saying that if a property owner is denied all economically viable use of his or her property, a taking has occurred and the Constitution requires that he or she get compensation.

Political or policy-oriented litigation is more prevalent in the appellate courts than in the trial courts and is most common in the U.S. Supreme Court. Ordinary compensatory litigation is often terminated early in the judicial process because the litigants find it more profitable to settle their dispute or accept the verdict of a trial court. However, litigants in political cases generally do little to advance their policy goals by gaining victories at the lower levels of the judiciary. Instead, they prefer the more widespread publicity that is attached to a decision by an appellate tribunal. Pursuing cases in the appellate courts is expensive. Therefore, many lawsuits that reach this level are supported in one way or another by interest groups.

INTEREST GROUPS IN THE JUDICIAL PROCESS

Although interest groups are probably better known for their attempts to influence legislative and executive branch decisions, they also pursue their policy goals in the courts. Some groups have found the judicial branch to be more receptive to their efforts than either of the other two branches of government. Interest groups that do not have the economic resources to mount an intensive lobbying effort in Congress or a state legislature may find it much easier to hire a lawyer and find some constitutional or statutory provision upon which to base a court case. Likewise, a small group with few registered voters among its members may lack the political clout to exert much influence on legislators and ex-

One of the most famous cases involving special interests was the 1925 "monkey trial," where the American Civil Liberties Union (ACLU) sent Clarence Darrow, left, to defend biology teacher John T. Scopes in his test of Tennessee's law banning the teaching of the theory of evolution. William Jennings Bryan, right, testified for the prosecution as a Bible expert.

During the 1950s and 1960s, interest group lawyers such as Thurgood Marshall, then chief counsel of the National Association for the Advancement of Colored People (NAACP), successfully persuaded the courts to support African Americans' struggle for their civil rights. Marshall here is shown with one of his clients, Autherine Lucy, expelled within days of becoming the first African American student to attend the University of Alabama, allegedly "for her own safety" in response to threats.

ecutive branch officials. Large memberships and political clout are not prerequisites for filing suits in the courts, however.

Interest groups may also turn to the courts because they find the judicial branch more sympathetic to their policy goals than the other two branches. Throughout the 1960s interest groups with liberal policy goals fared especially well in the federal courts. In addition, the public interest law firm concept gained prominence during this period. The public interest law firms pursue cases that serve the public interest in general — including cases in the areas of consumer rights, employment discrimination, occupational safety, civil liberties, and environmental concerns.

In the 1970s and 1980s conservative interest groups turned to the federal courts more frequently than they had before. This was in part a reaction to the successes of liberal interest groups. It was also due to the increasingly favorable forum that the federal courts provided for conservative viewpoints.

Interest group involvement in the judicial process may take several different forms depending upon the goals of the particular group. However, two principal tactics stand out: involvement in test cases and presentation of information before the courts through "amicus curiae" (Latin, meaning "friend of the court") briefs.

Test Cases

Because the judiciary engages in policy making only by rendering decisions in specific cases, one tactic of interest groups is to make sure that a case appropriate for obtaining its policy goals is brought before the court. In some instances this means that the interest group will initiate and sponsor the case by providing all the necessary resources. The best-known example of this type of sponsorship is *Brown v. Board of Education* (1954). In that case, although the suit against the Board of Education of Topeka, Kansas, was filed by the parents of Linda Brown, the National Association for the Advancement of Colored People (NAACP) supplied the legal help and money necessary to pursue the case all the way to the Supreme Court. Thurgood Marshall, who later became a U.S. Supreme Court justice, argued the suit on behalf of the plaintiff and the NAACP. As a result, the NAACP gained a victory through the Supreme Court's decision that segregation in the public schools violates the equal protection clause of the Fourteenth Amendment.

Interest groups may also provide assistance in a case initiated by someone else, but which nonetheless raises issues of importance to the group. A good example of this situation may be found in a freedom of religion case, *Wisconsin v. Yoder*. That case was initiated by the state of Wisconsin when it filed criminal complaints charging

Linda Brown, left, and her younger sister with their parents, who filed the landmark suit *Brown v. Board of Education* (1954) that led to the Supreme Court's decision that segregation in the public schools violates the equal protection clause of the Fourteenth Amendment.

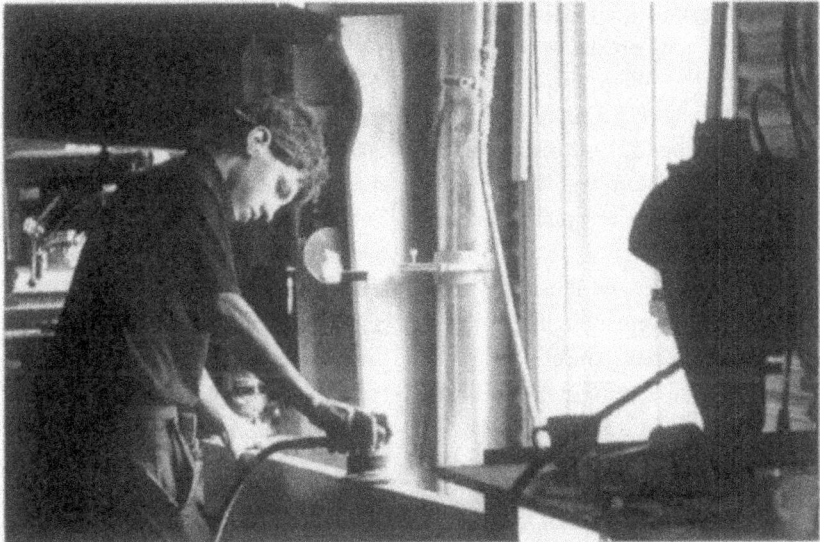

Abe Yoder, the Amish youth whose father, along with others of his faith, were charged by the state of Wisconsin with failure to send their children to school until the age of 16, as required by state law. In this freedom of religion case, interest groups came to the defense of the parents.

Jonas Yoder and others with failure to send their children to school until the age of 16 as required by state law. Yoder and the others, members of the Amish faith, believed that education beyond the eighth grade led to the breakdown of the values they cherished and to "worldly influences on their children."

An organization known as the National Committee for Amish Religious Freedom (NCARF) came to the defense of Yoder and the others. Following a decision against the Amish in the trial court, the NCARF appealed to a Wisconsin circuit court, which upheld the trial court's decision. An appeal was made to the Wisconsin Supreme Court, which ruled in favor of the Amish, saying that the compulsory school attendance law violated the free exercise of religion clause of the First Amendment. Wisconsin then appealed to the U.S. Supreme Court, which on May 15, 1972, sustained the religious objection that the NCARF had raised to the compulsory school attendance laws.

As these examples illustrate, interest group involvement in litigation has focused on cases concerning major constitutional issues that have reached the Supreme Court. Because only a small percentage of cases ever reaches the nation's highest court, however, most of the work of interest group lawyers deals with more routine work at the lower levels of the judiciary. Instead of fashioning major test cases for the appellate courts, these attorneys may simply be required to deal with the legal problems of their groups' clientele.

During the civil rights movement in the 1950s and 1960s, for example, public interest lawyers not only litigated major civil rights questions; they also defended African Americans and civil rights workers who ran into difficulties with the local authorities. These interest group attorneys, then, performed many of the functions of a specialized legal aid society: They provided legal representation to those involved in an important movement for social change. Furthermore, they performed the important function of drawing attention to the plight of African Americans by keeping cases before the courts.

Amicus Curiae Briefs

Submission of amicus curiae briefs is the easiest method by which interest groups can become involved in cases. This method allows a group to get its message before the court even though it does not control the case. Provided it has the permission of the parties to the case or the permission of the court, an interest group may submit an amicus brief to supplement the arguments of the parties. The filing of amicus briefs is a tactic used in appellate rather than trial courts, at both the federal and the state levels.

Sometimes these briefs are aimed at strengthening the position of one of the parties in the case. When the *Wisconsin v. Yoder* case was argued before the U.S. Supreme Court, the cause of the Amish was supported by amicus curiae briefs filed by the General Conference of Seventh Day Adventists, the National Council of Churches of Christ in the United States, the Synagogue Council of America, the American Jewish Congress, the National Jewish Commission on Law and Public Affairs, and the Mennonite Central Committee.

Sometimes friend-of-the-court briefs are used not to strengthen the arguments of one of the parties but to suggest to the court the group's own view of how the case should be re-solved. Amicus curiae briefs are often filed in an attempt to persuade an appellate court to either grant or deny review of a lower-court decision. A study of the U.S. Supreme Court found that the presence of amicus briefs significantly increased the chances that the Court would give full treatment to a case.

Unlike private interest groups, all levels of the government can submit amicus briefs without obtaining permission. The solicitor general of the United States is especially important in this regard, and in some instances the Supreme Court may invite the solicitor general to present an amicus brief.   ⚖

THE
CRIMINAL
COURT
PROCESS

A jury forewoman reads the verdict in court. The Sixth Amendment of the Constitution guarantees Americans the right to an impartial jury.

The criminal process begins when a law is first broken and extends through the arrest, indictment, trial, and appeal. There is no single criminal, or civil, court process in the United States. Instead, the federal system has a court process at the national level, and each state and territory has its own set of rules and regulations that affect the judicial process. Norms and similarities do exist among all of these governmental entities, and the discussion will focus primarily on these, but no two states have identical judicial systems and no state's system is identical to that of the national government.

THE NATURE AND SUBSTANCE OF CRIME

An act is not automatically a crime because it is hurtful or sinful. An action constitutes a true crime only if it specifically violates a criminal statute duly enacted by Congress, a state legislature, or some other public authority. A crime, then, is an offense against the state punishable by fine, imprisonment, or death. A crime is a violation of obligations due the community as a whole and can be punished only by the state. The sanctions of imprisonment and death cannot be imposed by a civil court or in a civil action (although a fine may be a civil or a criminal penalty).

In the United States most crimes constitute sins of commission, such as aggravated assault or embezzlement; a few consist of sins of omission, such as failing to stop and render aid after a traffic accident or failing to file an income tax return. The state considers some crimes serious, such as murder and treason, and this seriousness is reflected in the corresponding punishments, such as life imprisonment or the death penalty. The state considers others crimes only mildly reprehensible, such as double parking or disturbing the peace, and consequently punishments of a light fine or a night in the local jail are akin to an official slap on the wrist.

Some crimes, such as kidnapping or rape, constitute actions that virtually all citizens consider outside the sphere of acceptable human conduct, whereas other crimes constitute actions about which opinion would be divided. For example, an 1897 Michigan statute makes it illegal to curse in front of a child, and a Nebraska law forbids bingo games at church suppers. Other criminal statutes are plainly silly: In Wisconsin it is illegal to sing in a bar, and in Louisiana it is forbidden to appear drunk at a meeting of a literary society.

The most serious crimes in the United States are felonies. In a majority of the states a felony is any offense for which the penalty may be death (in states that allow it) or imprisonment in the penitentiary (a federal or state prison); all other offenses are misdemeanors or infractions. In other states, and under federal law, a felony is an offense for which the penalty may be death or imprisonment for a year or more. Thus, felonies are distinguished in some states according to the place where the punishment occurs; in some states and according to the federal government, the length of the sentence is the key factor. Examples of felonies include murder, forcible rape, and armed robbery.

Misdemeanors are regarded as petty crimes by the state, and their punishment usually consists of confinement in a city or county jail for less than a year. Public drunkenness, small-time gambling, and vagrancy are common examples of misdemeanor offenses. Some states have a third category of offense known as infractions. Often they include minor traffic offenses, such as parking violations, and the penalty is usually a small fine. Fines may also be part of the penalty for misdemeanors and felonies.

CATEGORIES OF CRIME

Five broad categories that comprise the primary criminal offenses in the United States today are conventional, economic, syndicated, political, and consensual.

Conventional Crimes

Property crimes make up the lion's share of the 31.3 million conventional crimes committed annually in the United States. Property crimes are distinguished by the government from crimes of violence, although the two

often go hand in glove. For example, the thief who breaks into a house and inadvertently confronts a resistant owner may harm the owner and thus be involved in more than just the property crime of burglary.

The less numerous, but more feared, conventional crimes are those against the person. These crimes of violence include murder and nonnegligent manslaughter, forcible rape, robbery, and aggravated assault.

Economic Crimes

There are four broad categories of economic crimes:

• Personal crimes consist of nonviolent criminal activity that one person inflicts on another with the hope of monetary gain. Examples include intentionally writing a bad check, cheating on one's income tax, and committing welfare fraud.

• Abuse of trust occurs when business or government employees violate their fidelity to their employer or clients and engage in practices such as commercial bribery, theft and embezzlement from the workplace, and filling out false expense accounts.

• Business crimes are crimes that are not part of the central purpose of the business enterprise but are incidental to (or in furtherance of) it. Misleading advertising, violations of the antitrust laws, and false depreciation figures computed for corporate income tax purposes are all business crimes.

• Con games are white-collar criminal activities committed under the guise of a business.

Syndicated, or Organized, Crimes

Syndicated crime is engaged in by groups of people and is often directed on some type of hierarchical basis. It represents an ongoing activity that is inexorably entwined with fear and corruption. Organized crime tends to focus on areas that are particularly lucrative, such as trafficking in illegal drugs, gambling, prostitution, and loan-sharking (money-lending at exorbitant interest rates and high repayment rates).

Political Crimes

Political crime usually constitutes an offense against the government: treason, armed rebellion, assassination of public officials, and sedition. However, the term has come to include crimes committed by the government against individual citizens, dissident groups, and foreign governments or nationals — for example, illegal wiretaps conducted by the government of politically dissident groups or the refusal of the military to investigate incidents of sexual harassment.

Consensual Crimes

So-called victimless crime, such as prostitution, gambling, illegal drug use, and unlawful sexual practices between consenting adults, is called consensual because both perpetrator and client desire the forbidden activity.

ELEMENTS OF A CRIME

Every crime has several distinct elements, and unless the state is able to demonstrate in court the existence of these essential elements there can be no conviction. Although the judicial process in the courtroom may not focus separately and distinctly on each of these elements, they are at least implicit throughout the entire

Syndicated crime is one of five broad categories that comprise the primary criminal offenses in the United States today. At this June 20, 2002, press conference, U.S. Attorney General for the Southern District of New York James Comey, left, and Kevin Donovan, right, assistant director of the New York FBI field office, announce the indictment of 14 alleged members of the Gambino organized crime family in New York.

process of duly convicting someone of a criminal offense.

A Law Defining the Crime and the Punishment

If an act is to be prohibited or required by the law, a duly constituted authority (usually Congress or a state legislature) must properly spell out the matter so that the citizenry can know in advance what conduct is prohibited or required. Lawmakers must also set forth the penalties to be imposed upon the individual who engages in the harmful conduct.

There are several corollaries to this general principle. One is that the U.S. Constitution forbids criminal laws that are ex post facto, that is, laws that declare certain conduct to be illegal after the conduct takes place. Likewise, the state may not pass bills of attainder, which are laws that single out a particular person or group of persons and declare that something is criminal for them but legal for everyone else. A final corollary is that a law defining a crime must be precise so that the average person can determine in advance what conduct is prohibited or required.

The Actus Reus

"Actus reus" is the Latin phrase meaning the criminal action committed by the accused that gives rise to the legal prosecution. The actus reus is the material element of the crime. This element may be the commission of an action that is forbidden (for instance,

assault and battery), or it may be the failure to perform an action that is required (for instance, a person's refusal to stop and render aid to a motor vehicle accident victim).

The Mens Rea

The "mens rea" (a Latin term) is the essential mental element of the crime. The U.S. legal system has always made a distinction between harm that was caused intentionally and harm that was caused by simple negligence or accident. Thus, if one person takes the life of another, the state does not always call it murder. If the killing was done with malice aforethought by a sane individual, it will likely be termed "murder in the first degree." But if the killing occurred in the passion of a barroom brawl, it would more likely be called "second-degree murder," which carries a lesser penalty. Reckless driving on the highway that results in the death of another would correspondingly be considered "negligent homicide" — a wrong, to be sure, but not as serious in the eyes of the state as the intentional killing of another.

An Injury or Result

A crime consists of a specific injury or a wrong perpetrated by one person against another. The crime may harm society at large, such as selling military secrets to a foreign government, or the injury may be inflicted upon an individual and, because of its nature, is considered to offend society as a whole. The nature of the injury, as with the mens rea, often determines the nature of the crime itself. For example, consider two drivers who have been cutting each other off in traffic. Finally they both stop their cars and come out fighting. Suppose one of them hits the other so hard he dies. The crime may be murder (of some degree). If the man does not die but suffers serious bodily harm, the crime is aggravated assault. If the injury is minor, the charge may be simple assault. Because the nature of the injury often determines the offense, it is frequently asserted that the nature of the injury is the key legal element of the crime.

Some actions may be criminal even though no injury is actually inflicted. Most crimes of criminal conspiracy fall into this category. For instance, if several persons were to plan to assassinate a judge or to bribe jurors in an attempt to keep a criminal from being convicted, the crime would be conspiracy to obstruct justice. This would be a crime even if the judge went unharmed and no money was ever passed to the jurors. All that is required is that the crime be planned and intended and that some specific, overt act be taken by one of the conspirators in furtherance of their plan (such as the purchase of a weapon or possession of a map of the route that the judge takes between his home and the courtroom).

A Causal Relationship Between the Action and the Resultant Injury

Before there can be a conviction for a criminal offense, the state must prove that the accused, acting in a natural and continuous sequence, produced the harmful situation. Usually proving a causal relationship is not difficult. If "Bill" stabs "John" with a knife and inflicts a minor wound, there is no doubt that Bill is guilty of assault with a deadly weapon. But what if John does not obtain proper medical care for the wound, develops an infection, and subsequently dies? Is Bill now guilty of manslaughter or murder? Or what if after being stabbed, John stumbles across a third party and causes injury to her? Is Bill to blame for this, too?

Resolution of questions such as these are often difficult for judges and juries. The law requires that all circumstances be taken into account. The accused can be convicted only if the state can prove that his or her conduct is the direct, immediate, or determining cause of the resultant harm to the victim.

PROCEDURES BEFORE A CRIMINAL TRIAL

Before a criminal trial can be held, federal and state laws require a series of procedures and events. Some of these stages are mandated by the U.S. Constitution and state constitutions, some by court decisions, and others by legislative enactments. Custom and tradition often account for the rest. Although the exact nature of these procedural events varies from federal to state practice — and from one state to another — there are similarities throughout the country. These procedures, however, are not as automatic or routine as they might appear; rather, the judicial system's decision makers exercise discretion at all stages according to their values, attitudes, and views of the world.

The Arrest

The arrest is the first substantial contact between the state and the accused. The U.S. legal system provides for two basic types of arrest — those with a warrant and those without. A warrant is issued after a complaint, filed by one person against another, has been presented and reviewed by a magistrate who has found probable cause for the arrest. Arrests without a warrant occur when a crime is committed in the presence of a police officer or when an officer has probable cause to believe that someone has committed (or is about to commit) a crime. Such a belief must later be established in a sworn statement or testimony. In the United States up to 95 percent of all arrests are made without a warrant.

An officer's decision whether to make an arrest is far from simple or automatic. To be sure, the officer who witnesses a murder will make an arrest on the spot if possible. But most lawbreaking incidents are not that simple

or clear-cut, and police officials possess — and exercise — wide discretion about whether to take someone into custody. Sufficient resources are simply not available to the police for them to proceed against all activities that Congress and the legislatures have forbidden. Consequently, discretion must be exercised in determining how to allocate the time and resources that do exist. Police discretion is at a maximum in several areas.

Trivial Offenses. Many police manuals advise their officers that when minor violations of the law are concerned, a warning is a more appropriate response than an arrest. Traffic violations, misconduct by juveniles, drunkenness, gambling, and vagrancy all constitute less serious crimes and entail judgment calls by police.

Victim Will Not Seek Prosecution. Nonenforcement of the law is also the rule in situations where the victim of a crime will not cooperate with the police in prosecuting a case. In the instance of minor property crimes, for example, the victim is often satisfied if restitution occurs and the victim cannot afford the time to testify in court. Unless the police have expended considerable resources in investigating a particular property crime, they are generally obliged to abide by the victim's wishes.

When the victim of a crime is in a continuing relationship with the criminal, the police often decline to make an arrest. Such relationships include landlord and tenant, one neighbor and another, and, until recently, husband and wife. In this last case, however, heightened awareness of domestic violence has had a significant impact on police procedures.

Rape and child molestation constitute another major category of crimes for which there are often no arrests because the victims will not or cannot cooperate with the police. Oftentimes the victim is personally acquainted with, or related to, the criminal, and the fear of reprisals or of ugly publicity inhibits the victim from pressing a complaint.

Victim Also Involved in Misconduct.
When police officers perceive that the victim of a crime is also involved in some type of improper or questionable conduct, the officers frequently opt not to make an arrest.

Appearance Before a Magistrate

After a suspect is arrested for a crime, he or she is booked at the police station; that is, the facts surrounding the arrest are recorded and the accused may be fingerprinted and photographed. Next the accused appears before a lower-level judicial official whose title may be judge, magistrate, or commissioner. Such an appearance is supposed to occur "without unnecessary delay"; in 1991 the U.S. Supreme Court ruled that

police may detain an individual arrested without a warrant for up to 48 hours without a court hearing on whether the arrest was justified.

This appearance in court is the occasion of several important events in the criminal justice process. First, the accused must have been informed of the precise charges and must be informed of all constitutional rights and guarantees. Among others, these rights include those of the now famous *Miranda v. Arizona* decision handed down in 1966 by the Supreme Court. The accused "must be warned prior to any questioning that he has the right to remain silent, that anything he says can be used against him in a court of law, that he has the right to the presence of an attorney, and that if he cannot afford an attorney one will be appointed for him prior to any questioning." (Such warnings must also be given by the arresting officer if the officer questions the suspect about the crime.) In some states the accused must be informed about other rights that are provided for in the state's Bill of Rights, such as the right to a speedy trial and the right to confront hostile witnesses.

Second, the magistrate will determine whether the accused is to be released on bail and, if so, what the amount of bail is to be. Constitutionally, the only requirement for the amount is that it shall not be "excessive." Bail is considered to be a privilege — not a right — and it may be denied altogether in capital punishment cases for which the evidence of guilt is strong or if the magistrate believes that the accused will flee from prosecution no matter what the amount of bail. An alternative to bail is to release the defendant on recognizance, basically on a pledge by the defendant to return to court on the appointed date for trial.

In minor cases the accused may be asked to plead guilty or not guilty. If the plea is guilty, a sentence may be pronounced on the spot. If the defendant pleads not guilty, a trial date is scheduled. However, in the typical serious (felony) case, the next primary duty of the magistrate is to determine whether the defendant requires a preliminary hearing. If such a hearing is appropriate, the matter is adjourned by the prosecution and a subsequent stage of the criminal justice process begins.

The Grand Jury Process or the Preliminary Hearing

At the federal level all persons accused of a crime are guaranteed by the Fifth Amendment to have their cases considered by a grand jury. However, the Supreme Court has refused to make this right binding on the states. Today only about half of the states use grand juries; in some of these, they are used for only special types of cases. Those states that do not use grand juries employ a preliminary hearing or an examining trial. (A few states use both procedures.) Regardless of which method is used, the primary purpose of this stage in the criminal justice process is to determine whether there

---

WARNING AS TO YOUR RIGHTS

You are under arrest. Before we ask you any questions, you must understand what your rights are.

You have the right to remain silent. You are not required to say anything to us at any time or to answer any questions. Anything you say can be used against you in court.

You have the right to talk to a lawyer for advice before we question you and to have him with you during questioning.

If you cannot afford a lawyer and want one, a lawyer will be provided for you.

If you want to answer questions now without a lawyer present you will still have the right to stop answering at any time. You also have the right to stop answering at any time until you talk to a lawyer. **P-4475**

Since 1966, police have had to advise suspects about their rights prior to any interrogation. They use the so-called "Miranda Warning," named after Ernesto Miranda, who was granted a retrial because he was not advised about his rights.

is probable cause for the accused to be subjected to a formal trial.

The Grand Jury. Grand juries consist of 16 to 23 citizens, usually selected at random from the voter registration lists, who render decisions by a majority vote. Their terms may last anywhere from one month to one year, and some may hear more than a thousand cases during their term. The prosecutor alone presents evidence to the grand jury. Not only are the accused and his or her attorney absent from the proceedings, but usually they also have no idea which grand jury is hearing the case or when. If a majority believes probable cause exists, then an indictment, or true bill, is brought. Otherwise the result is a no bill.

Historically two arguments have been made in favor of grand juries. One is that grand juries serve as a check on a prosecutor who might be using the office to harass an innocent person for political or personal reasons. Ideally an unbiased group of citizens would interpose themselves between an unethical prosecutor and the defendant. A second justification for grand juries is to make sure that the district attorney has secured enough evidence to warrant the trouble and expense — for both the state and the accused — of a full-fledged trial.

The Preliminary Hearing. In the majority of states that have abolished the grand jury system, a preliminary hearing is used to determine whether there is probable cause for the accused to be bound over for trial. At this hearing the prosecution presents its case, and the accused has the right to cross-examine witnesses and to produce favorable evidence. Usually the defense elects not to fight at this stage of the criminal process; in fact, a preliminary hearing is waived by the defense in the vast majority of cases.

If the examining judge determines that there is probable cause for a trial or if the preliminary hearing is waived, the prosecutor must file a bill of information with the court where the trial will be held. This serves to outline precisely the charges that will be adjudicated in the new legal setting.

The Arraignment

Arraignment is the process in which the defendant is brought before the judge in the court where he or she is to be tried to respond to the grand jury indictment or the prosecutor's bill of information. The prosecutor or a clerk usually reads in open court the charges that have been brought against the accused. The defendant is informed that he or she has a constitutional right to be represented by an attorney and that a lawyer will be appointed without charge if necessary.

The defendant has several options about how to plead to the charges. The most common pleas are guilty and not guilty. But the accused may also plead not guilty by reason of insanity, former jeopardy (having been tried on the same charge at another time), or "nolo contendere" (from the Latin, no contest). Nolo contendere means that the accused does not deny the facts of the case but claims that he or she has not committed any crime, or it may mean that the defendant does not understand the charges. The nolo contendere plea can be entered only with the consent of the judge (and sometimes the prosecutor as well). Such a plea has two advantages. It may help the accused save face vis-à-vis the public because he or she can later claim that technically no guilty verdict was reached even though a sentence or a fine may have been imposed. Also, the plea may spare the defendant from certain civil penalties that might follow a guilty plea (for example, a civil suit that might follow from conviction for fraud or embezzlement).

If the accused pleads not guilty, the judge will schedule a date for a trial. If the plea is guilty, the defendant may be sentenced on the spot or at a later date set by the judge. Before the court will accept a guilty plea, the judge must certify that the plea was made voluntarily and that the defendant was aware of the implications of the plea. A guilty plea is to all intents and purposes the equivalent to a formal verdict of guilty.

The Possibility of a Plea Bargain

At both the state and federal levels at least 90 percent of all criminal cases never go to trial. That is because before the trial date a bargain has been struck between the prosecutor and the defendant's attorney concerning the official charges to be brought and the nature of the sentence that the state will recommend to the court. In effect, some form of leniency is promised in exchange for a guilty plea.

Because plea bargaining virtually seals the fate of the defendant before trial, the role of the judge is simply to ensure that the proper legal and constitutional procedures have been followed. There are three (not mutually exclusive) types of plea bargains.

Reduction of Charges. The most common form of agreement between a prosecutor and a defendant is a reduction of the charge to one less serious than that supported by the evidence. This exposes the criminal to a substantially reduced range of sentence possibilities. A second reason for a defendant to plead guilty to a reduced charge is to avoid a record of conviction for an offense that carries a social stigma. Another possibility is that the defendant may wish to avoid a felony record altogether and would be willing to plead guilty to almost any misdemeanor offered by the prosecutor rather than face a felony charge.

Deletion of Tangent Charges. A second form of plea bargain is the agreement of the district attorney to drop other charges pending against an individual. There are two variations on this theme. One is an agreement not to prosecute "vertically" — that is, not to prosecute more serious charges filed against the individual. The second type of agreement is to dismiss "horizontal" charges; that is to dismiss additional indictments for the same crime pending against the accused.

Another variation of this type of plea bargaining is the agreement in which a repeater clause is dropped from an indictment. At the federal level and in many states, a person is considered a habitual criminal upon the third conviction for a violent felony anywhere in the United States. The mandatory sentence for the habitual criminal is life imprisonment. In state courts the habitual criminal charge often is dropped in exchange for a plea of guilty.

Another plea bargain of this type is the agreement in which indictments in different courts are consolidated into one court in order that the sentences may run concurrently. As indictments or preliminary hearing rulings are handed down in many jurisdictions, they are placed on a trial docket on a rotation system. This means that a defendant charged with four counts of forgery and one charge of possession of a forged instrument might be placed on the docket of five different courts. Generally it is common practice in such multicourt districts to transfer all of a person's indictments to the first court listed. This gives the presiding judge the discretion of allowing all of the defendant's sentences to run concurrently.

Sentence Bargaining. A third form of plea bargaining concerns a plea of guilty from the defendant in exchange for a prosecutor's agreement to ask the judge for a lighter sentence. The strength of the sentence negotiation is based upon the realities of the limited resources of the judicial system. At the state level, at least, prosecutors are able to promise the defendant a fairly specific sentence with confidence that the judge will accept the recommendation. If the judge were not to do so, the prosecutor's credibility would quickly begin to wane, and many of the defendants who had been pleading guilty would begin to plead not guilty and take their chances in court. The result would be a gigantic increase in court dockets that would overwhelm the judicial system and bring it to a standstill. Prosecutors and judges understand this reality, and so do the defense attorneys.

Constitutional and Statutory Restrictions on Plea Bargaining. At both the state and federal levels, the requirements of due process of law mean that plea bargains must be made voluntarily and with comprehension. This means that the defendant must be admonished by the court of the consequences of a guilty plea (for example, the defendant waives all opportunities to change his or her mind at a later date), that the accused must be sane, and that, as one state puts it, "It must plainly appear that the defendant is uninfluenced by any consideration of fear or by any persuasion, or delusive hope of pardon prompting him to confess his guilt."

For the first two types of plea bargains — reduction of charges and deletion of tangent charges — some stricter standards govern the federal courts. One is that the judge may not actually participate in the process of plea bargaining; at the state level judges may play an active role in this process. Likewise, if a plea bargain has been made between the U.S. attorney and the defendant, the government may not renege on the agreement. If the federal government does so, the federal district judge must withdraw the guilty plea. Finally, the Federal Rules of Criminal Procedure require that before a guilty plea may be accepted, the prosecution must present a summary of the evidence against the accused, and the judge must agree that there is strong evidence of the defendant's guilt.

Arguments For and Against Plea Bargaining.

For the defendant the obvious advantage of the bargain is that he or she is treated less harshly than would be the case if the accused were convicted and sentenced under maximum conditions. Also, the absence of a trial often lessens publicity on the case, and because of personal interests or social pressures, the accused may wish to avoid the length and publicity of a formal trial. Finally, some penologists (professionals in the field of punishment and rehabilitation) argue that the first step toward rehabilitation is for a criminal to admit guilt and to recognize his or her problem.

Plea bargaining also offers some distinct advantages for the state and for society as a whole. The most obvious is the certainty of conviction, because no matter how strong the evidence may appear, an acquittal is always a possibility as long as a trial is pending. Also, the district attorney's office and judges are saved an enormous amount of time and effort by their not having to prepare and preside over cases in which there is no real contention of innocence or that are not suited to the trial process. Finally, when police officers are not required to be in court testifying in criminal trials, they have more time to devote to preventing and solving crimes.

Plea bargains do have a negative side as well. The most frequent objection to plea bargaining is that the defendant's sentence may be based upon nonpenological grounds. With the large volume of cases making plea bargaining the rule, the sentence often bears no relation to the specific facts of the case, to the correctional needs of the criminal, or to society's legitimate interest in vigorous prosecution of the case. A second defect is that if plea bargaining becomes the norm of a particular system, then undue pressure may be placed upon even innocent persons to plead guilty. Studies have shown that, in some jurisdictions, the less the chance for conviction, the harder the bargaining may be because the prosecutor wants to get at least some form of minimal confession out of the accused.

A third disadvantage of plea bargaining is the possibility of the abuse called overcharging — the process whereby the prosecutor brings charges against the accused more severe than the evidence warrants, with the hope that this will strengthen his or her hand in subsequent negotiations with the defense attorney.

Another flaw with the plea bargaining system is its very low level of visibility. Bargains between prosecutor and defense attorney are not made in open court presided over by a neutral jurist and for all to observe. Instead, they are more likely made over a cup of coffee in a basement courthouse cafeteria where the conscience of the two lawyers is the primary guide.

Finally, the system has the potential to circumvent key procedural and constitutional rules of evidence. Because the prosecutor need not present any evidence or witnesses in court, a bluff may result in a conviction even though the case might not be able to pass the muster of the due process clause. The defense may be at a disadvantage because the rules of discovery (the laws that allow the defense to know in detail the evidence the prosecution will present) in some states limit the defense counsel's case preparation to the period after the plea bargain has occurred. Thus the plea bargain may deprive the accused of basic constitutional rights.

The Adversarial Process

The adversarial model is based on the assumption that every case or controversy has two sides to it: In criminal cases the government claims a defendant is guilty while the defendant contends innocence; in civil cases the plaintiff asserts that the person he or she is suing has caused some injury while the respondent denies responsibility. In the courtroom each party provides his or her side of the story as he or she sees it. The theory (or hope) underlying this model is that the truth will emerge if each party is given unbridled opportunity to present the full panoply of evidence, facts, and arguments before a neutral and attentive judge (and jury).

The lawyers representing each side are the major players in this courtroom drama. The judge acts more as a passive, disinterested referee whose primary role is to keep both sides within the accepted rules of legal procedure and courtroom decorum. The judge eventually determines which side has won in accordance with the rules of evidence, but only after both sides have had a full opportunity to present their case.

PROCEDURES DURING A CRIMINAL TRIAL

Assuming that no plea bargain has been struck and the accused maintains his or her innocence, a formal trial will take place. This is a right guaranteed by the Sixth Amendment to all Americans charged with federal crimes and a right guaranteed by the various state constitutions — and by the Fourteenth Amendment — to all persons charged with state offenses. The accused is provided many constitutional and statutory rights during the trial. The following are the primary rights that are binding on both the federal and state courts.

Basic Rights Guaranteed During the Trial Process

The Sixth Amendment says, "In all criminal prosecutions, the accused shall enjoy the right to a speedy and public trial." The Founders emphasized the word speedy so that an accused would not languish in prison for a long time prior to the trial or have the determination of his or her fate put off for an unduly long period of time. But how soon is speedy? Although this word has been defined in various ways by the Supreme Court, Congress gave new meaning to the term when it passed the Speedy Trial Act of 1974. The act mandated time

limits, ultimately reaching 100 days, within which criminal charges must either be brought to trial or dismissed. Most states have similar measures on the statute books, although the precise time period varies from one jurisdiction to another. By "public trial" the Founders meant to discourage the notion of secret proceedings whereby an accused could be tried without public knowledge and whisked off to some unknown detention camp.

The Sixth Amendment also guarantees Americans the right to an impartial jury. At the least this has meant that the prospective jurors must not be prejudiced one way or the other before the trial begins. For example, a potential juror may not be a friend or relative of the prosecutor or the crime victim; nor may someone serve who believes that anyone of the defendant's race or ethnic ancestry is "probably the criminal type." What the concept of an impartial jury of one's peers has come to mean in practice is that jurors are to be selected randomly from the voter registration lists — supplemented in an increasing number of jurisdictions by lists based on automobile registrations, driver's licenses, telephone books, welfare rolls, and so on. Although this system does not provide a perfect cross-section of the community, because not all persons are registered to vote, the Supreme Court has said that this method is good enough. The High Court has also ruled that no class of persons (such as African

Americans or women) may be systematically excluded from jury service.

Besides being guaranteed the right to be tried in the same locale where the crime was committed and to be informed of the charges, defendants have the right to be confronted with the witnesses against them. They have the right to know who their accusers are and what they are charging so that a proper defense may be formulated. The accused is also guaranteed the opportunity "to have the Assistance of Counsel for his defense." Prior to the 1960s this meant that one had this right (at the state level) only for serious crimes and only if one could pay for an attorney. However, because of a series of Supreme Court decisions, the law of the land guarantees one an attorney if tried for any crime that may result in a prison term, and the government must pay for the legal defense for an indigent defendant. This is the rule at both the national and state levels.

The Fifth Amendment to the U.S. Constitution declares that no person shall "be subject for the same offence to be twice put in jeopardy of life and limb." This is the double jeopardy clause and means that no one may be tried twice for the same crime by any state government or by the federal government. It does not mean, however, that a person may not be tried twice for the same action if that action has violated both national and state laws. For example, someone who robs a federally chartered bank in New Jersey runs afoul of both federal and state law. That person could be legally tried and acquitted for that offense in a New Jersey court and subsequently be tried for that same action in federal court.

Another important right guaranteed to the accused at both the state and federal levels is not to "be compelled in any criminal case to be a witness against himself." This has been interpreted to mean that the fact that someone elects not to testify on his or her own behalf in court may not be used against the person by judge and jury. This guarantee serves to reinforce the principle that under the U.S. judicial system the burden of proof is on the state; the accused is presumed innocent until the government proves otherwise beyond a reasonable doubt.

Finally, the Supreme Court has interpreted the guarantee of due process of law to mean that evidence procured in an illegal search and seizure may not be used against the accused at trial. The source of this so-called exclusionary rule is the Fourth Amendment to the U.S. Constitution; the Supreme Court has made its strictures binding on the states as well. The Court's purpose was to eliminate any incentive the police might have to illegally obtain evidence against the accused.

Selection of Jurors

If the accused elects not to have a bench trial — that is, not to be tried and sentenced by a judge alone — his or her fate will be determined by a jury. At the federal level 12 persons must render a unanimous verdict. At the state level such criteria apply only to the most serious offenses. In many states a jury may consist of fewer than 12 persons and render verdicts by other than unanimous decisions.

A group of potential jurors is summoned to appear in court. They are questioned in open court about their general qualifications for jury service in a process known as "voir dire" (from Old French, meaning "to say the truth"). The prosecutor and the defense attorney ask general and specific questions of the potential jurors. Are they citizens of the state? Can they comprehend the English language? Have they or anyone in their family ever been tried for a criminal offense? Have they read about or formed any opinions about the case at hand?

In conducting the voir dire, the state and the defense have two goals. The first is to eliminate all members of the panel who have an obvious reason why they might not render an impartial decision in the case. Common examples might be someone who is excluded by law from serving on a jury, a juror who is a friend or relative of a participant in the trial, and someone who openly admits a strong bias in the case at hand. Objections to jurors in this category are known as challenges for cause, and the number of such challenges is unlimited. It is the judge who determines whether these challenges are valid.

The second goal that the opposing attorneys have in questioning prospective jurors is to eliminate those who they believe would be unfavorable to their side even though no overt reason is apparent for the potential bias. Each side is allowed a number of peremptory challenges — requests to the court to exclude a prospective juror with no reason given. Most states customarily give the defense more peremptory challenges than the prosecution. At the federal level one to three challenges per jury are usually permitted each side, depending on the nature of the offense; as many as 20 are allowed in capital cases. The use of peremptory challenges is more of an art than a science and is usually based on the hunch of the attorneys.

In the past attorneys were able to exclude potential jurors via the peremptory challenge for virtually any reason whatsoever. However, in recent years the Supreme Court has interpreted the Fourteenth Amendment's equal protection clause to restrict this discretion by prohibiting prosecutors from using their challenges to exclude African Americans or women from serving on a criminal jury.

The process of questioning and challenging prospective jurors continues until all those duly challenged for cause are eliminated, the peremptory challenges are either used up or waived, and a jury of 12 (six in some states) has been created. In some states alternate jurors are also chosen. They attend the trial but participate in deliberations only if one of the original jurors is unable to continue in the proceedings. Once the panel has been selected, they are sworn in by the judge or the clerk of the court.

Opening Statements

After the formal trial begins, both the prosecution and the defense make an opening statement (although in no state is the defense compelled to do so). Long and detailed statements are more likely to be made in jury trials than in bench trials. The purpose of opening statements is to provide members of the jury — who lack familiarity with the law and with procedures of criminal investigation — with an outline of the major objectives of each side's case, the evidence that is to be presented, the witnesses that are to be called, and what each side seeks to prove. If the opening statements are well presented, the jurors will find it easier to grasp the meaning and significance of the evidence and testimony. The usual procedure is for the state to make its opening statement first and for the defense to follow with a statement about how it will refute that case.

The Prosecution's Case

After the opening statements the prosecutor presents the evidence amassed by the state against the accused. Evidence is generally of two types — physical evidence and the testimony of witnesses. The physical evidence may include things such as bullets, ballistics tests, fingerprints, handwriting samples, blood and urine tests, and other documents or items that serve as physical aids. The defense may object to the admission of any of these tangible items and will, if successful, have the item excluded from consideration. If defense challenges are unsuccessful, the physical evidence is labeled by one of the courtroom personnel and becomes part of the official record.

Most evidence at criminal trials takes the form of testimony of witnesses. The format is a question-and-answer procedure whose purpose is to elicit very specific information in an orderly fashion. The goal is to present only evidence that is relevant to the immediate case at hand and not to give confusing or irrelevant information or illegal evidence that might result in a mistrial (for example, evidence that the accused had a prior conviction for an identical offense).

After each witness the defense attorney has the right to cross-examine. The goal of the defense will be to impeach the testimony of the prosecution witness — that is, to discredit it. The attorney may attempt to confuse, fluster, or anger the witness, causing him or her to lose self-control and begin providing confusing or conflicting testimony. A prosecution witness' testimony may also be impeached if defense witnesses who contradict the version of events suggested by the state are subsequently presented. Upon completion of the cross-examination, the prosecutor may conduct a redirect examination, which serves to clarify or correct some telling point made during the cross-examination. After the state has presented all its evidence and witnesses, it rests its case.

The Case for the Defense

The presentation of the case for the defense is similar in style and format to that of the prosecution. Tangible evidence is less common in the defense's case, and most of the evidence will be that of witnesses who are prepared to rebut or contradict the prosecution's arguments. The witnesses are questioned by the defense attorney in the same style as those in the prosecution case. Each defense witness may in turn be cross-examined by the district attorney, and then a redirect examination is in order.

The difference between the case for the prosecution and the case for the defense lies in their obligation before the law. The defense is not required by law to present any new or additional evidence or any witnesses at all. The defense may consist merely of challenging the credibility or the legality of the state's evidence and witnesses. The defense is not obligated to prove the innocence of the accused; it need show only that the state's case is not beyond a reasonable doubt. The defendant need not even take the stand. (However, if he or she elects to do so, the accused faces the same risks of cross-examination as any other witness.)

After the defense has rested its case, the prosecution has the right to present rebuttal evidence. In turn, the defense may offer a rejoinder known as a surrebuttal. After that, each side delivers closing arguments. Oftentimes this is one of the more dramatic episodes in the trial because each side seeks to sum up its case, condense its strongest arguments, and make one last appeal to the jury. New evidence may not be presented at this stage, and the arguments of both sides tend to ring with emotion and appeals to values that transcend the immediate case. The prosecutor may talk about the crime problem in general, about the need for law and order, and about the need not to let compassion for the accused get in the way of empathy for the crime victim. The defense attorney, on the other hand, may remind the jurors "how we have all made mistakes in this life" or argue that in a free, democratic society any doubt they have should be resolved in favor of the accused. The prosecution probably avoids emotionalism more than the defense attorney, however, because many jury verdicts have been reversed on appeal after the district attorney injected prejudicial statements into the closing statements.

Role of the Judge During the Trial

The judge's role in the trial, although very important, is a relatively passive

Prosecutors and police display a seizure of more than $45 million worth of heroin and cocaine. Illegal drug traffic belongs under either one of two categories of crime: organized crime and consensual crime, also known as victimless crime, because both the perpetrator and the client desire the forbidden activity.

Witnesses and physical evidence form the principal elements of the prosecution's case in most trials. Left: Tampa Police Department investigators take fingerprint samples in an attempt to trace an accused terrorist. Above: An expert witness points to a chart of the parking lot where an alleged crime took place.

one. He or she does not present any evidence or take an active part in the examination of the witnesses. The judge is called upon to rule on the many motions of the prosecutor and of the defense attorney regarding the types of evidence that may be presented and the kinds of questions that may be asked of the witnesses. In some jurisdictions the judge is permitted to ask substantive questions of the witnesses and also to comment to the jury about the credibility of the evidence that is presented; in other states the judge is constrained from such activity. Still, the American legal tradition has room for a variety of judicial styles that depend on the personality, training, and wisdom of individual judges.

First and foremost, the judge is expected to play the part of a disinterested party whose primary job is to see to it that both sides are allowed to present their cases as fully as possible within the confines of the law. If judges depart from the appearance or practice of being fair and neutral parties, they run counter to fundamental tenets of American jurisprudence and risk having their decisions overturned by an appellate court.

Although judges do for the most part play such a role, the backgrounds and values of the jurists also affect their decisions in the close calls — when they are called upon to rule on a motion for which the arguments are about equally strong or on a point of law that is open to a variety of interpretations.

Role of the Jury During the Trial

The jurors' role during the trial is passive. Their job is to listen attentively to the cases presented by the opposing attorneys and then come to a decision based solely on the evidence that is set forth. They are ordinarily not permitted to ask questions either of the witnesses or of the judge, nor are they allowed to take notes of the proceedings. This is not because of constitutional or statutory prohibitions but primarily because it has been the traditional practice of courts in America.

In recent years, however, many judges have allowed jurors to become more involved in the judicial arena. Chicago's Chief U.S. District Court Judge John F. Grady has for over a decade permitted jurors in his courtroom to take notes. At least four U.S. appellate courts have given tacit approval to the practice of juror participation in questioning witnesses, as long as jurors are not permitted to blurt out queries in the midst of trial and attorneys are given a chance to object to specific questions before they are posed to witnesses. In some states a few trial judges have allowed jurors to take fairly active roles in the trial. Still, at both state and federal levels the role of the jury remains basically passive.

Instructions to the Jury

Although the jury's job is to weigh and assess the facts of the case, the judge must instruct the jurors about the meaning of the law and how the law is to be applied. Because many cases are overturned on appeal as a result of faulty jury instructions, judges tend to take great care that the wording be technically and legally correct.

All jury instructions must have some basic elements. One is to define for the jurors the crime with which the accused is charged. This may involve giving the jurors a variety of options about what kind of verdict to bring. For example, if one person has taken the life of another, the state may be trying the accused for first-degree murder. Nevertheless, the judge may be obliged to acquaint the jury with the legal definition of second-degree murder or manslaughter if it should determine that the defendant was the killer but did not act with malice aforethought.

The judge must also remind the jury that the burden of proof is on the state and that the accused is presumed to be innocent. If, after considering all the evidence, the jury still has a reasonable doubt as to the guilt of the accused, it must bring in a not guilty verdict.

Finally, the judge usually acquaints the jurors with a variety of procedural matters: how to contact the judge if they have questions, the order in which they must consider the charges

if there are more than one, who must sign the official documents that express the verdict of the jury. After the instructions are read to the jury (and the attorneys for each side have been given an opportunity to offer objections), the jurors retreat into a deliberation room to decide the fate of the accused.

The Jury's Decision

The jury deliberates in complete privacy; no outsiders observe or participate in its debate. During their deliberation jurors may request the clarification of legal questions from the judge, and they may look at items of evidence or selected segments of the case transcript, but they may consult nothing else — no law dictionaries, no legal writings, no opinions from experts. When it has reached a decision by a vote of its members, the jury returns to the courtroom to announce its verdict. If it has not reached a decision by nightfall, the jurors are sent home with firm instructions neither to discuss the case with others nor read about the case in the newspapers. In very important or notorious cases, the jury may be sequestered by the judge, which means that its members will spend the night in a local hotel away from the public eye.

If the jury becomes deadlocked and cannot reach a verdict, it may report that fact to the judge. In such an event the judge may insist that the jury continue its effort to reach a ver-

Defendants in the photos to the left and above are shown awaiting the jury's verdict and listening to the judge's announcement of the verdict. Once the verdict is reached, the judge has several weeks to determine the penalty, based on the principle that the punishment should fit the crime. Bottom left, a prisoner is led back to his cell.

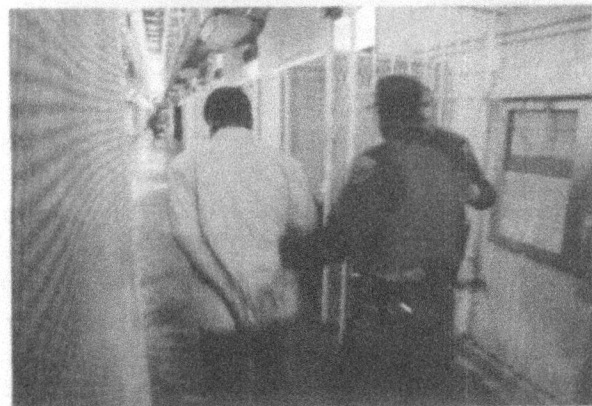

dict. Or, if the judge is convinced that the jury is in fact hopelessly deadlocked, he or she may dismiss the jury and call for a new trial.

Research studies indicate that most juries dealing with criminal cases make their decisions fairly quickly. Almost all juries take a vote soon after they retire to their chambers in order to see how divided, or united, they are. In 30 percent of the cases it takes only one vote to reach a unanimous decision. In 90 percent of the remainder, the majority on the first ballot eventually wins out. Hung juries — those in which no verdict can be reached — tend to occur only when a large minority existed on the first ballot.

Scholars have also learned that juries often reach the same verdict that the judge would have, had he or she been solely responsible for the decision. One large jury study asked judges to state how they would have decided jury cases over which they presided. The judge and jury agreed in 81 percent of the criminal cases (about the same as in civil cases). In 19 percent of the criminal cases the judge and jury disagreed, with the judge showing a marked tendency to convict where the juries had acquitted.

When the members of the jury do finally reach a decision, they return to the courtroom and their verdict is announced in open court, often by the jury foreman. At this time either the prosecutor or the defense attorney often asks that the jury be polled —

that is, that each juror be asked individually if the general verdict actually reflects his or her own opinion. The purpose is to determine whether each juror supports the overall verdict or whether he or she is just caving in to group pressure. If the polling procedure reveals that the jury is indeed not of one mind, it may be sent back to the jury room to continue deliberations; in some jurisdictions a mistrial may be declared. If a mistrial is declared, the case may be tried again before another jury. There is no double jeopardy because the original jury did not agree on a verdict. If the jury's verdict is not guilty, the defendant is discharged on the spot and is free to leave the courtroom.

PROCEDURES AFTER A CRIMINAL TRIAL

At the close of the criminal trial, generally two stages remain for the defendant if he or she has been found guilty: sentencing and an appeal.

Sentencing

Sentencing is the court's formal pronouncement of judgment upon the defendant at which time the punishment or penalty is set forth.

At the federal level and in most states, sentences are imposed by the judge only. However, in several states the defendant may elect to be sentenced by either a judge or a jury, and in capital cases states generally require that no death sentence shall be imposed unless it is the determination of 12 unanimous jurors. In some states after a jury finds someone guilty, the jury deliberates a second time to determine the sentence. In several states a new jury is empaneled expressly for sentencing. At this time the rules of evidence are more relaxed, and the jury may be permitted to hear evidence that was excluded during the actual trial (for example, the previous criminal record of the accused).

After the judge pronounces the sentence, several weeks customarily elapse between the time the defendant is found guilty and the time when the penalty is imposed. This interval permits the judge to hear and consider any posttrial motions that the defense attorney might make (such as a motion for a new trial) and to allow a probation officer to conduct a presentence investigation. The probation officer is a professional with a background in criminology, psychology, or social work, who makes a recommendation to the judge about the length of the sentence to be imposed. The probation officer customarily examines factors such as the background of the criminal, the seriousness of the crime committed, and the likelihood that the criminal will continue to engage in illegal activity. Judges are not required to follow the probation officer's recommendation, but it is still a major factor in the judge's calculus as to what the sentence shall be. Judges are presented with a variety of alternatives and a range of sentences when it comes to punishment for the criminal. Many of these alternatives involve the concept of rehabilitation and call for the assistance of professionals in the fields of criminology and social science.

The lightest punishment that a judge can hand down is that of probation. This is often the penalty if the crime is regarded as minor or if the judge believes that the guilty person is not likely to engage in additional criminal activity. If a probated sentence is handed down, the criminal may not spend any time in prison as long as the conditions of the probation are maintained. Such conditions might include staying away from convicted criminals, not committing other crimes, or with increasing frequency, performing some type of community service. If a criminal serves out his or her probation without incident, the criminal record is usually wiped clean and in the eyes of the law it is as if no crime had ever been committed.

If the judge is not disposed toward probation and feels that jail time is in order, he or she must impose a prison sentence that is within a range prescribed by law. The reason for a range of years instead of an automatically assigned number is that the law recognizes that not all crimes and criminals are alike and that in principle the punishment should fit the crime.

In an effort to eliminate gross disparities in sentencing, the federal government and many states have attempted to develop sets of precise guidelines to create greater consistency among judges. At the national level this effort was manifested by the enactment of the Sentencing Reform Act of 1987, which established guidelines to structure the sentencing process.

Congress provided that judges may depart from the guidelines only if they find an aggravating or mitigating circumstance that the commission did not adequately consider. Although the congressional guidelines do not specify the kinds of factors that could constitute grounds for departure from the sentencing guidelines, Congress did state that such grounds could not include race, gender, national origin, creed, religion, socioeconomic status, drug dependence, or alcohol abuse.

The states, too, have a variety of programs for avoiding vast disparities in judges' sentences. By 1995, 22 states had created commissions to establish sentencing guidelines for their judges, and as of late 1997 such guidelines were in effect in 17 states. Likewise, almost all of the states have now enacted mandatory sentencing laws that require an automatic, specific sentence upon conviction of certain crimes — particularly violent crimes, crimes in which a gun was used, or crimes perpetrated by habitual offenders.

Despite the enormous impact that judges have on the sentence, they do not necessarily have the final say on the matter. Whenever a prison term is set by the judge, it is still subject to the parole laws of the federal government and of the states. Thus parole boards (and sometimes the president and governors who may grant pardons or commute sentences) have the final say about how long an inmate actually stays in prison.

An Appeal

At both the state and federal levels everyone has the right to at least one appeal upon conviction of a felony, but in reality few criminals avail themselves of this privilege. An appeal is based on the contention that an error of law was made during the trial process. Such an error must be reversible as opposed to harmless. An error is considered harmless if its occurrence had no effect on the outcome of the trial. A reversible error, however, is a serious one that might have affected the verdict of the judge or jury. For example, a successful appeal might be based on the argument that evidence was improperly admitted at trial, that the judge's instructions to the jury were flawed, or that a guilty plea was not voluntarily made. However, appeals must be based on questions of procedure and legal interpretations, not on factual determinations of the defendant's guilt or innocence as such. Furthermore, under most circumstances one cannot appeal the length of one's sentence in the United States (as long as it was in the range prescribed by law).

Criminal defendants do have some degree of success on appeal about 20 percent of the time, but this does not mean that the defendant goes free. The usual practice is for the appellate court to remand the case (send it back down) to the lower court for a new trial. At that point the prosecution must determine whether the procedural errors in the original trial can be overcome in a second trial and whether it is worth the time and effort to do so. A second trial is not considered to be double jeopardy, since the defendant has chosen to appeal the original conviction.

The media and others concerned with the law often call attention to appellate courts that turn loose seemingly guilty criminals and to convictions that are reversed on technicalities. Surely this does happen, and one might argue that this is inevitable in a democratic country whose legal system is based on fair play and the presumption of the innocence of the accused. However, about 90 percent of all defendants plead guilty, and this plea virtually excludes the possibility of an appeal. Of the remaining group, two-thirds are found guilty at trial, and only a small percentage of these appeal. Of those who do appeal, only about 20 percent have any measurable degree of success. Of those whose convictions are reversed, many are found guilty at a subsequent trial. Thus the number of persons convicted of crimes who are subsequently freed because of reversible court errors is a small fraction of 1 percent.   ⚖

THE
CIVIL
COURT
PROCESS

Multnomah (Oregon) County
Circuit Judge Roosevelt Robinson
polls the jury about the verdict in a
civil law case involving tort law,
specifically, a suit brought against
a corporation for defective
products.

Civil actions are separate and distinct from criminal proceedings. This chapter focuses on civil courts: how civil law differs from criminal law, the most important categories of civil law, alternatives to trials, and a step-by-step look at the civil trial process.

THE NATURE AND SUBSTANCE OF CIVIL LAW

The American legal system observes several important distinctions between criminal and civil law. Criminal law is concerned with conduct that is offensive to society as a whole. Civil law pertains primarily to the duties of private citizens to each other. In civil cases the disputes are usually between private individuals, although the government may sometimes be a party in a civil suit. Criminal cases always involve government prosecution of an individual for an alleged offense against society.

In a civil case the court attempts to settle a particular dispute between the parties by determining their legal rights. The court then decides upon an appropriate remedy, such as awarding monetary damages to the injured party or issuing an order that directs one party to perform or refrain from a specific act. In a criminal case the court decides whether the defendant is innocent or guilty. A guilty defendant may be punished by a fine, imprisonment, or both.

In some instances the same act may give rise to both a criminal proceeding and a civil suit. Suppose that "Joe" and "Pete," two political scientists attending a convention in Atlanta, are sharing a taxi from the airport to their downtown hotel. During the ride they become involved in a heated political discussion. By the time the taxi stops at their hotel, the discussion has become so heated that they get into a physical confrontation. If Pete strikes Joe in the ribs with his briefcase as he gets out of the taxi, Pete may be charged with criminal assault. In addition, Joe might file a civil suit against Pete in an effort to obtain a monetary award sufficient to cover his medical expenses.

Civil cases far outnumber criminal cases in both the federal and state courts, although they generally do not attract the same media attention as criminal trials. Still, they often raise important policy questions and cover a broad range of disagreements in society. Judicial scholar Herbert Jacob summarizes the breadth of the civil law field in *Justice in America*: "Every broken agreement, every sale that leaves a dissatisfied customer, every uncollected debt, every dispute with a government agency, every libel and slander, every accidental injury, every marital breakup, and every death may give rise to a civil proceeding."

Thus, virtually any dispute between two or more persons may provide the basis for a civil suit. The number of suits is huge, but most of them fall into one of five basic categories.

THE MAIN CATEGORIES OF CIVIL LAW

The five main categories of civil law are contract law, tort law, property law, the law of succession, and family law.

Contract Law

Contract law is primarily concerned with voluntary agreements between two or more people. Some common examples include agreements to perform a certain type of work, to buy or sell goods, and to construct or repair homes or businesses. Basic to these agreements are a promise by one party and a counter promise by the other party, usually a promise by one party to pay money for the other party's services or goods. For example, assume that "Mr. Burns" and "Ms. Colder" enter into an agreement whereby Colder agrees to pay Burns $125 if he will cut and deliver a cord of oak firewood to her home on December 10. If Burns does not deliver the wood on that date, he has breached the contract and Colder may sue him for damages.

Although many contracts are relatively simple and straightforward, some complex fields also build on contract law or contract ideas. One such field is commercial law, which focuses primarily on sales involving credit or the installment plan. Commercial law also deals with checks, promissory notes, and other negotiable financial instruments.

Bankruptcy and creditors' rights are important areas in contract law. Above, a jet belonging to American Airlines, which in 2003 narrowly averted a bankruptcy filing.

Another closely related field is bankruptcy and creditors' rights. Bankrupt individuals or businesses may go through a process that essentially wipes the slate clean and allows the person filing for bankruptcy to begin again. The bankruptcy process is also designed to ensure fairness to creditors. Bankruptcy law has been a major concern of legislators for several years, and a large number of special bankruptcy judges are now attached to the U.S. district courts.

The final area is the insurance contract, which is important because of its applicability to so many people. The insurance industry is regulated by government agencies and subject to its own distinct rules.

Tort Law

Tort law may generally be described as the law of civil wrongs. It concerns conduct that causes injury and fails to measure up to some standard set by society.

Actions for personal injury or bodily injury claims are at the heart of tort law, and automobile accidents have traditionally been responsible for a large number of these claims. One of the most rapidly growing subfields of tort law is product liability. This category has become an increasingly effective way to hold corporations accountable for injuries caused by defective foods, toys, appliances, automobiles, drugs, or a host of other products.

Perhaps one reason for the growth in product liability cases is a change in the standard of proof. Traditionally, negligence (generally defined as carelessness or the failure to use ordinary care, under the particular circumstances revealed in the lawsuit) must be proven before one person is able to collect damages for injuries caused by someone else. However, some have argued that for many years reliance on the negligence concept has been declining, especially in product liability cases. In its place, the courts often use a strict liability standard, which means that a victim can recover even if there was no negligence and even if the manufacturer was careful.

Another reason commonly suggested for the growth in the number of product liability cases is the size of jury awards when the decision favors the plaintiff. Jury awards for damages may be of two types: compensatory and punitive. Compensatory damages are intended to cover the plaintiff's actual loss, such as repair costs, doctor bills, and hospital expenses. Punitive (or exemplary) damages are designed, instead, to punish the defendant or serve as a warning against such behavior in the future.

As a result of concern over large jury awards and the increasing number of so-called frivolous cases, government officials, corporate executives, interest groups, and members of the legal community have called for legislation aimed at tort reform.

Throughout the 1990s a number of states enacted a variety of tort reform measures. The American Tort Reform Association, which serves as an advocate of tort reform, reports that states have limited awards for noneconomic damages, modified their laws governing punitive damages, or enacted statutes penalizing plaintiffs who file frivolous lawsuits.

Another rapidly growing subfield of tort law is medical malpractice. The number of medical malpractice claims has increased even as great advances have been made in medicine. Two ongoing problems in contemporary medicine are the increased risk imposed by new treatments and the impersonal character of specialists and hospitals. Patients today have high expectations, and when a doctor fails them, their anger may lead to a malpractice suit.

Courts generally use the traditional negligence standard rather than the strict liability doctrine in resolving medical malpractice suits. This means that the law does not attempt to make doctors guarantee successful treatment, but instead tries to make the doctor liable if the patient can prove that the physician failed to perform in a manner consistent with accepted methods of medical practice. The notion of acceptable practice varies from state to state, and such questions must be resolved by the courts on a case-by-case basis. However, customarily a presumption is made that the conduct of professionals, including doctors, is reasonable in nature. This means that to prevail against the doctor in court, the injured patient needs at least the testimony of one or more expert witnesses stating that the doctor's conduct was not reasonable.

Property Law

A distinction has traditionally been made between real property and personal property. The former normally refers to real estate — land, houses, and buildings — and has also included growing crops. Almost everything else is considered personal property, including such things as money, jewelry, automobiles, furniture, and bank deposits.

According to Lawrence M. Friedman in *American Law*, "As far as the law is concerned, the word property means primarily real property; personal property is of minor importance." No single special field of law is devoted to personal property. Instead, personal property is generally considered under the rubric of contract law, commercial law, and bankruptcy law.

Property rights have always been important in the United States, but today property rights are more complex than mere ownership of something. The notion of property now includes, among several other things, the right to use that property.

One important branch of property law today deals with land use controls. The most common type of land use

Product liability is one of the most rapidly growing subfields of tort law, with many manufacturers increasingly being held liable even when they were careful. Above, product liability attorney Ralph G. Patino displays a tire that his client claimed separated from its casing and caused a serious accident — one of many claims that led the Firestone Company to recall millions of its tires in 2000.

Property law — the right to use and the right to acquire property — was the principal question behind the Federal Communications Commission's 2003 review of whether to ease regulations on media ownership for corporations.

restriction is zoning, a practice whereby local laws divide a municipality into districts designated for different uses. For instance, one neighborhood may be designated as residential, another as commercial, and yet another as industrial.

Early zoning laws were challenged on the ground that restrictions on land use amounted to a taking of the land by the city in violation of the Constitution, which says, "Nor shall private property be taken for public use without just compensation." In a sense, zoning laws do take from the owners of land the right to use their property in any way they see fit. Nonetheless, courts have generally ruled that zoning laws are not regarded as a taking in violation of the Constitution. Today, zoning is a fact of life in cities and towns of all sizes throughout the United States. City planners and other city officials recognize zoning ordinances as necessary to the planned and orderly growth of urban areas.

The Law of Succession

The law of succession considers how property is passed along from one generation to another. The American legal system recognizes a person's right to dispose of his or her property as he or she wishes. One common way to do this is to execute a will. If a person leaves behind a valid will, the courts will enforce it. However, if someone leaves no will (or has improperly drawn it up), then the person has died intestate, and the state must dispose of the property.

The state's disposition of the property is carried out according to the fixed scheme set forth in the state statutes. By law, intestate property passes to the deceased person's heirs — that is, to his or her nearest relatives. Occasionally a person who dies intestate has no living relatives. In that situation the property escheats, or passes, to the state in which the deceased resided. State statutes often prohibit the more remote relatives, such as second cousins and great uncles and aunts, from inheriting.

Increasingly, Americans are preparing wills to ensure that their property is disposed of according to their wishes, not according to a scheme determined by the state. A will is a formal document. It must be very carefully drafted, and in most states it must be witnessed by at least two persons.

Family Law

Family law concerns such matters as marriage, divorce, child custody, and children's rights. It clearly touches the lives of a great number of Americans each year.

The conditions necessary for entering into a marriage are spelled out by state law. These laws traditionally cover the minimum age of the parties, required blood tests or physical examinations, mental conditions of the parties, license and fee requirements, and waiting periods.

The termination of a marriage was once very rare. In the early 19th century some states granted divorces only through special acts of the legislature; one state, South Carolina, simply did not allow divorce. In the other states divorces were granted only when one party proved some grounds for divorce. In other words, divorces were available only to innocent parties whose spouses were guilty of such things as adultery, desertion, or cruelty.

The 20th century saw an enormous change in divorce laws. The movement was away from restrictive laws and toward no-fault divorce. This trend was the result of two factors. First, for many years there was an increasing demand for divorces. Second, the stigma once attached to divorced persons all but disappeared.

The no-fault divorce system means that the parties simply explain that irreconcilable differences exist between them and that the marriage is no longer viable. The no-fault divorce system has put an end to the adversarial nature of divorce proceedings.

Not so easily solved are some of the other problems that may result from an ended marriage. Child custody battles, disputes over child support payments, and disagreements

Two children await the results of a custody decision by the Manhattan Family Court. Custody disputes have become more common as a result of no-fault divorce, and courts increasingly have to decide which parent will get custody.

over visitation rights find their way into court on a regular basis. Custody disputes are probably more common and more contentious today than before no-fault divorce. The child's needs come first, and courts no longer automatically assume that this means granting custody to the mother. Fathers are increasingly being granted custody, and it is also now common for courts to grant joint custody to the divorced parents.

THE COURTS AND OTHER INSTITUTIONS CONCERNED WITH CIVIL LAW

Disagreements are common in the daily lives of Americans. Usually these disagreements can be settled outside the legal system. Sometimes they are so serious, however, that one of the parties sees no alternative but to file a lawsuit.

Deciding Whether to Go to Court

Every year thousands of potential civil cases are resolved without a trial because the would-be litigants settle their problems in another way or because the prospective plaintiff decides not to file suit. When faced with a decision to call upon the courts, to try to settle differences, or to simply forget the problem, many people resort to a simple cost-benefit analysis. That is, they weigh the costs associated with a trial against the benefits they are likely to gain if they win.

Alternative Dispute Resolution

In practice few persons make use of the entire judicial process. Instead, most cases are settled without resort to a full-fledged trial. In civil cases, a trial may be both slow and expensive. In many areas the backlogs are so enormous that it takes three to five years for a case to come to trial. In addition, civil trials may be exceedingly complex.

Often, the expense of a trial is enough to discourage potential plaintiffs. The possibility of losing always exists. The possibility of a long wait also always exists, even if a plaintiff wins, before the judgment is satisfied — that is, if it is ever completely satisfied. In other words, a trial may simply create a new set of problems for the parties concerned. For all these reasons, more and more discussion has been heard about alternative methods of resolving disputes.

From major corporations to attorneys to individuals, support for alternative dispute resolution (ADR) has been growing. Corporate America is interested in avoiding prolonged and costly court battles as the only way to settle complex business disputes. In addition, attorneys are more frequently considering alternatives such as mediation and arbitration where there is a need for faster resolution of cases or confidential treatment of certain matters. And individual citizens are increasingly turning to local mediation services for help in resolving family disputes, neighborhood quarrels, and consumer complaints.

Alternative dispute resolution processes are carried out under a variety of models. These models are commonly classified as "private, court-referred, and court-annexed, but the latter two together often are called court-connected," writes Susan L. Keita in the *Handbook of Court Administration and Management*. In other words, some private ADR processes function independently of the courts. A court-referred ADR process is one that operates outside the court itself but still has some relationship to the court. The court administers the ADR process in a court-annexed program. Depending on the model and the issue, "ADR processes may be voluntary or mandatory; they may be binding or allow appeals from decisions rendered; and they may be consensual, adjudicatory, or some hybrid of the two," according to Keita. Some commonly used ADR processes are mediation, arbitration, neutral fact-finding, mini-trial, summary jury trial, and private judging.

Mediation. Mediation is a private, confidential process in which an impartial person helps the disputing parties identify and clarify issues of concern and reach their own agreement. The mediator does not act as a judge. Instead, the parties themselves maintain control of the final settlement.

Mediation is especially appropriate for situations in which the disputants have an ongoing relationship, such as disputes between family members, neighbors, employers and employees, and landlords and tenants. Mediation is also useful in divorce cases because it changes the procedure from one of confrontation to one of cooperation. Child custody and visitation rights are frequently resolved through mediation as well. And in many areas, personal injury and property claims involving insurance companies are settled through mediation.

Arbitration. The arbitration process is similar to going to court. After listening to both parties in a dispute, an impartial person called an arbitrator decides how the controversy should be resolved. There is no judge or jury. Instead, the arbitrator selected by both parties makes the final decision. Arbitrators are drawn from all different types of professional backgrounds and frequently volunteer their time to help people resolve their problems.

Disputants choose arbitration because it saves time and money and is more informal than a court hearing. Most arbitrations are completed in four months or less, as compared with six months to several years for court decisions.

Arbitration is used privately to resolve a variety of consumer complaints. Examples include disputes over poor automobile repairs, problems with the return of faulty merchandise, and overcharging for services. Arbitration is also being used in court-referred and court-annexed processes to resolve several types of disputes, including business, commercial, and employment disputes.

Neutral Fact-Finding. Neutral fact-finding is an informal process whereby an agreed-upon neutral party is asked to investigate a dispute. Usually, the dispute involves complex or technical issues. The neutral third party analyzes the disputed facts and issues his or her findings in a nonbinding report or recommendation.

This process can be particularly useful in handling allegations of racial or gender discrimination within a company because such cases often provoke strong emotions and internal dissension. If both parties are employees of the same company, conflicts of interest could interfere with a supervisor or manager's ability to conduct an impartial investigation of alleged discrimination. To avoid the appearance of unfairness, a company may turn to a neutral third party in hopes of reaching a settlement all the employees can respect.

Mini-Trial. In a mini-trial each party presents its position in a trial-like fashion before a panel that consists of selected representatives for both parties and neutral third parties. Every panel has one neutral advisor. Mini-

trials are designed to help define the issues and develop a basis for realistic settlement negotiations. The representatives from the two sides present an overview of their positions and arguments to the panel. As a result, each party becomes more knowledgeable about the other party's position. Having heard each side's presentation, the panel, including the advisor, meets to develop a compromise solution. The neutral advisor may also issue an advisory opinion regarding the merits of the case. This advisory opinion is nonbinding unless the parties have agreed in writing beforehand to be bound by it.

The primary benefit of a mini-trial is that both parties have an opportunity to develop solutions. It also means that each has representation and access to detailed information.

Summary Jury Trial. A summary jury trial involves a court-managed process that takes place after a case has been filed, but before it reaches trial. In a summary jury trial each party presents its arguments to a jury (normally six persons). An overview of each side's argument as well as abbreviated opening and closing arguments are presented. Attorneys are typically given a short amount of time (an hour or less) for their presentations. They are limited to the presentation of information that would be admissible at trial. No testimony is taken from sworn witnesses, and proceedings are generally not recorded. Because the proceedings are nonbinding, rules of procedure and evidence are more flexible than in a normal trial.

The jury hands down an advisory, nonbinding decision based on the arguments presented. In this setting, the verdict is designed to give the attorneys and their clients insight into their cases. It may also suggest a basis for settlement of the dispute. If the dispute is not resolved during or immediately following the summary jury trial proceeding, a pretrial conference is held before the court to discuss settlement.

One of the major advantages of a summary jury trial is the time involved. A summary jury trial is typically concluded in less than a day compared to several days or weeks for full-fledged trials.

Private Judging. This method of alternative dispute resolution makes use of retired judges who offer their services for a fee. Advocates claim that there are several advantages. First, the parties are able to select a person with the right qualifications and experience to handle the matter. Second, the parties can be assured that the matter will be handled when first scheduled and not be continued because the court's calendar is too crowded. Finally, the cost can be less than that incurred in full litigation. Critics of private judging, however, are concerned by the high fees charged by some retired

judges. A California appellate court, for instance, has noted that some sitting judges are leaving the bench in order to earn more money as private judges.

Specialized Courts

The state court systems are frequently characterized by a number of specialized courts that are set up to handle specific types of civil cases. Domestic relations courts are often established to deal with such matters as divorce, child custody, and child support. In many jurisdictions, probate courts handle the settlement of estates and the contesting of wills.

Perhaps the best known of the specialized courts are the small-claims courts. These courts have jurisdiction to handle cases when the money being sued for is not above a certain amount. The amount varies by jurisdiction but the maximum is usually $500 or $1,000. Small-claims courts allow less complex cases to be resolved more informally than in most other trial courts. Filing fees are low, and the use of attorneys is often discouraged, making small-claims court affordable for the average person.

Administrative Bodies

A number of government agencies have also established administrative bodies with quasi-judicial authority to handle certain types of cases. At the federal level, for example, agencies such as the Federal Trade Commission and the Federal Communications Commission carry out an adjudication of sorts within their respective spheres of authority. An appeal of the ruling of one of these agencies may be taken to a federal court of appeals.

At the state level, a common example of an administrative body that aids in the resolution of civil claims is a workers' compensation board. This board determines whether an employee's injury is job-related and thus whether the person is entitled to workers' compensation payments. Many state motor vehicle departments have hearing boards to make determinations about revoking driver's licenses. Another type of administrative board commonly found in the states rules on civil rights matters and cases of alleged discrimination.

THE CIVIL TRIAL PROCESS

A number of disputes are resolved through some method of alternative dispute resolution, in a specialized court, or by an administrative body. However, a large number of cases each year still manage to find their way into a civil court.

Generally speaking, the adversarial process used in criminal trials is also used in civil trials, with just a few important differences. First, a litigant must have standing. This concept means simply that the person initiating the suit must have a personal stake in the outcome of the controversy. Otherwise, there is no real controversy

between the parties and thus no actual case for the court to decide.

A second major difference is that the standard of proof used in civil cases is a preponderance of the evidence, not the more stringent beyond-a-reasonable-doubt standard used in criminal cases. A preponderance of the evidence is generally taken to mean that there is sufficient evidence to overcome doubt or speculation. It clearly means that less proof is required in civil cases than in criminal cases.

A third major difference is that many of the extensive due process guarantees that a defendant has in a criminal trial do not apply in a civil proceeding. For example, neither party is constitutionally entitled to counsel. The Seventh Amendment does guarantee the right to a jury trial in lawsuits "where the value in controversy shall exceed $20." Although this amendment has not been made applicable to the states, most states have similar constitutional guarantees.

Filing a Civil Suit

The person initiating the civil suit is known as the plaintiff, and the person being sued is the defendant or the respondent. A civil action is known by the names of the plaintiff and the defendant, such as Jones v. Miller. The plaintiff's name appears first. In a typical situation, the plaintiff's attorney pays a fee and files a complaint or petition with the clerk of the proper court. The complaint states the facts on which the action is based, the damages alleged, and the judgment or relief being sought.

The decision about which court should actually hear the case involves the concepts of jurisdiction and venue: Jurisdiction deals with a court's authority to exercise judicial power, and venue means the place where that power should be exercised.

Jurisdictional requirements are satisfied when the court has legal authority over both the subject matter and the person of the defendant. This means that several courts can have jurisdiction over the same case. Suppose, for example, that a resident of Dayton, Ohio, is seriously injured in an automobile accident in Tennessee when the car he is driving is struck from the rear by a car driven by a resident of Kingsport, Tennessee. Total damages to the Ohio driver and car come to about $80,000. A state trial court in Ohio has subject matter jurisdiction, and Ohio can in all likelihood obtain jurisdiction over the defendant. In addition, the state courts of Tennessee probably have jurisdiction. Federal district courts in both Ohio and Tennessee also have jurisdiction because diversity of citizenship exists and the amount in controversy is over $75,000. Assuming that jurisdiction is the only concern, the plaintiff can sue in any of these courts.

Heavy media coverage often prompts defense attorneys to move for a change of venue so as to avoid prejudicing their client's case, for instance, in auto accidents caused by drunk drivers.

The determination of proper venue may be prescribed by statute based on avoiding possible prejudice, or it may simply be a matter of convenience. The federal law states that proper venue is the district in which either the plaintiff or defendant resides, or the district where the injury occurred. State venue statutes vary somewhat, but they usually provide that where land is involved, proper venue is the county where the land is located. In most other instances venue is the county where the defendant resides.

Venue questions may also be related to the perceived or feared prejudice of either the judge or the prospective jury. Attorneys sometimes object to trials being held in a particular area for this reason and may move for a change of venue. Although this type of objection is perhaps more commonly associated with highly publicized criminal trials, it is also found in civil trials.

Once the appropriate court has been determined and the complaint has been filed, the court clerk will attach a copy of the complaint to a summons, which is then issued to the defendant. The summons may be served by personnel from the sheriff's office, a U.S. marshal, or a private process-service agency.

The summons directs the defendant to file a response, known as a pleading, within a certain period of time (usually 30 days). If the defen-dant does not do so, then he or she may be subject to a default judgment.

These simple actions by the plaintiff, clerk of the court, and a process server set in motion the civil case. What happens next is a flurry of activities that precedes an actual trial and may last for several months. Approximately 75 percent of cases are resolved without a trial during this time.

Pretrial Activities

Motions. Once the summons has been served on the defendant, a number of motions can be made by the defense attorney. A motion to quash requests that the court void the summons on the ground that it was not properly served. For example, a defendant might contend that the summons was never delivered personally as required by state law.

Two types of motions are meant to clarify or to object to the plaintiff's petition. A motion to strike requests that the court excise, or strike, certain parts of the petition because they are prejudicial, improper, or irrelevant. A motion to make more definite asks the court to require the plaintiff to be more specific about the complaints.

A fourth type of motion often filed in a civil case is a motion to dismiss. This motion may argue that the court lacks jurisdiction, or it may insist that the plaintiff has not presented a legally sound basis for action against the defendant even if the allegations are true.

The Answer. If the complaint survives the judge's rulings on the motions, then the defendant submits an answer to the complaint. The response may contain admissions, denials, defenses, and counterclaims. When an admission is contained in an answer, there is no need to prove that fact during the trial. A denial, however, brings up a factual issue to be proven during the trial. A defense says that certain facts set forth in the answer may bar the plaintiff from recovering damages.

The defendant may also create a separate action known as a counterclaim. If the defendant thinks that a cause of action against the plaintiff arises from the same set of events, then he or she must present the claim to the court in response to the plaintiff's claim. The plaintiff may file a reply to the defendant's answer. In that reply, the plaintiff may admit, deny, or defend against the allegations of fact contained in the counterclaim.

Discovery. The U.S. legal system provides for discovery procedures; that is, each party is entitled to information in the possession of the other. There are several tools of discovery:

• A deposition is testimony of a witness taken under oath outside the court. The same question-and-answer format as in the courtroom is used. All parties to the case must be notified that the deposition is to be taken so that their attorneys may be present to cross-examine the witness.

• Interrogatories are written questions that must be answered under oath. Interrogatories can be submitted only to the parties in the case, not to witnesses. They are used to obtain descriptions of evidence held by the opposing parties in the suit.

• Production of documents may be requested by one of the parties in the suit if they wish to inspect documents, writings, drawings, graphs, charts, maps, photographs, or other items held by the other party.

• If there are questions about the physical or mental condition of one of the parties, the court may order that person to submit to an examination by a physician.

The Pretrial Conference. Before going to court, the judge may call a pretrial conference to discuss the issues in the case informally with the opposing attorneys. The general practice is to allow only the judge and the lawyers to attend the conference, which is normally held in the judge's chambers.

At this meeting, the judge and the attorneys try to come to agreement on uncontested factual issues, which are known as stipulations. The purpose of stipulations is to make the actual trial more efficient by reducing the number of issues that must be argued in court. The attorneys also share with each other a list of witnesses and documents that are part of each case.

Lawyers and judges may also use the pretrial conference to try to settle the case. Some judges actively work to bring about a settlement so the case does not have to go to trial.

The Civil Trial

Selection of Jury. The right to a jury trial in a civil suit in a federal court is guaranteed by the Seventh Amendment of the U.S. Constitution. State constitutions likewise provide for such a right. A jury trial may be waived, in which case the judge decides the matter. Although the jury traditionally consists of 12 persons, today the number varies. Most of the federal district courts now use juries of fewer than 12 persons in civil cases. A majority of states also authorize smaller juries in some or all civil trials.

As in criminal trials, jurors must be selected in a random manner from a fair cross-section of the community. A large panel of jurors is called to the courthouse, and when a case is assigned to a court for trial, a smaller group of prospective jurors is sent to a particular courtroom.

Following the voir dire examination, which may include challenges to certain jurors by the attorneys, a jury to hear the particular case will be seated. Lawyers may challenge a prospective juror for cause, in which case the judge must determine whether the person challenged is impartial. Each side may also exercise a certain number of peremptory challenges — excusing a juror without

The Seventh Amendment of the Constitution and state constitutions guarantee the right to a jury trial in civil suits. As a result, many citizens such as these women from Macomb County, Michigan, are called to serve as jurors.

stating any reason. However, the U.S. Supreme Court has ruled that the equal protection guarantee of the Fourteenth Amendment prohibits the use of such challenges to disqualify jurors from civil trials because of their race or gender. Peremptory challenges are fixed by statute or court rule and normally range from two to six.

Opening Statements. After the jury has been chosen, the attorneys present their opening statements. The plaintiff's attorney begins. He or she explains to the jury what the case is about and what the plaintiff's side expects to prove. The defendant's lawyer can usually choose either to make an opening statement immediately after the plaintiff's attorney finishes or to wait until the plaintiff's case has been completely presented. If the defendant's attorney waits, he or she will present the entire case for the defendant continuously, from opening statement onward. Opening statements are valuable because they outline the case and make it easier for the jury to understand the evidence as it is presented.

Presentation of the Plaintiff's Case. In the normal civil case, the plaintiff's side is first to present and attempt to prove its case to the jury and last to make closing arguments. In presenting the case, the plaintiff's lawyer will normally call witnesses to testify and produce documents or other exhibits.

When a witness is called, he or she will undergo direct examination by the plaintiff's attorney. Then the defendant's attorney will have the opportunity to ask questions or cross-examine the witness. The Arizona Supreme Court recently took steps to help jurors do a better job of making decisions in civil cases. Among other things, the state's highest court voted to allow jurors to pose written questions to witnesses through the judge. Other states are considering implementing Arizona's new practice. Following the cross-examination, the plaintiff's lawyer may conduct a redirect examination, which may then be followed by a second cross-examination by the defendant's lawyer.

Generally speaking, witnesses may testify only about matters they have actually observed; they may not express their opinions. However, an important exception to this general rule is that expert witnesses are specifically called upon to give their opinions in matters within their areas of expertise.

To qualify as an expert witness, a person must possess substantial knowledge about a particular field. Furthermore, this knowledge must normally be established in open court. Both sides often present experts whose opinions are contradictory. When this happens, the jury must ultimately decide which opinion is the correct one.

When the plaintiff's side has presented all its evidence, the attorney rests the case.

Motion for Directed Verdict. After the plaintiff's case has been rested, the defendant will often make a motion for a directed verdict. With the filing of this motion, the defendant is saying that the plaintiff has not proved his or her case and thus should lose. The judge must then decide whether the plaintiff could win at this point if court proceedings were to cease. Should the judge determine that the plaintiff has not presented convincing enough evidence, he or she will sustain the motion and direct the verdict for the defendant. Thus the plaintiff will lose the case. The motion for a directed verdict is similar to the pretrial motion to dismiss.

Presentation of the Defendant's Case. If the motion for a directed verdict is overruled, the defendant then presents evidence. The defendant's case is presented in the same way as the plaintiff's case. That is, there is direct examination of witnesses and presentation of documents and other exhibits. The plaintiff has the right to cross-examine witnesses. Redirect and recross questions may follow.

Plaintiff's Rebuttal. After the presentation of the defendant's case, the plaintiff may bring forth rebuttal evidence, which is aimed at refuting the defendant's evidence.

Answer to Plaintiff's Rebuttal. The defendant's lawyer may present evidence to counter the rebuttal evidence. This rebuttal-and-answer pattern may continue until the evidence has been exhausted.

Closing Arguments. After all the evidence has been presented, the lawyers make closing arguments, or summations, to the jury. The plaintiff's attorney speaks both first and last. That is, he or she both opens the argument and closes it, and the defendant's lawyer argues in between. In this stage of the process each attorney attacks the opponent's evidence for its unreliability and may also attempt to discredit the opponent's witnesses. In doing so, the lawyers often wax eloquent or deliver an emotional appeal to the jury. However, the arguments must be based upon facts supported by the evidence and introduced at the trial.

Instructions to the Jury. Assuming that a jury trial has not been waived, the instructions to the jury follow the conclusion of the closing arguments. The judge informs the jury that it must base its verdict on the evidence presented at the trial. The judge's instructions also inform the jurors about the rules, principles, and standards of the particular legal concept involved. In civil cases, a finding for the plaintiff is based on a preponderance of the evidence. This means that the jurors must weigh the evidence presented during the trial and determine in their minds that the greater weight of the evidence, in merit and in worth, favors the plaintiff.

The Verdict. The jury retires to the seclusion of the jury room to conduct its deliberations. The members must reach a verdict without outside contact. In some instances the deliberations are so long and detailed that the jurors must be provided meals and sleeping accommodations until they can reach a verdict. The verdict, then, represents the jurors' agreement after detailed discussions and analyses of the evidence. Sometimes the jury deliberates in all good faith but cannot reach a verdict. When this occurs, the judge may declare a mistrial. This means that a new trial may have to be conducted.

After the verdict is reached, the jury is conducted back into open court, where it delivers its verdict to the judge. The parties are informed of the verdict. It is then customary for the jury to be polled — the jurors are individually asked by the judge whether they agree with the verdict.

Post-trial Motions. Once the verdict has been reached, a dissatisfied party may pursue a variety of tactics. The losing party may file a motion for judgment notwithstanding the verdict. This type of motion is granted when the judge decides that reasonable persons could not have rendered the verdict the jury reached.

The losing party may also file a motion for a new trial. The usual basis for this motion is that the verdict goes against the weight of the evidence. The judge will grant the motion on this ground if he or she agrees that the evidence presented simply does not support the verdict reached by the jury. A new trial may also be granted for a number of other reasons: excessive damages, grossly inadequate damages, the discovery of new evidence, and errors in the production of evidence, to name a few.

In some cases the losing party also files a motion for relief from judgment. This type of motion may be granted if the judge finds a clerical error in the judgment, discovers some new evidence, or determines that the judgment was induced by fraud.

Judgment and Execution. A verdict in favor of the defendant ends the trial, but a verdict for the plaintiff requires another stage in the process. There is no sentence in a civil case, but there must be a determination of the remedy or damages to be assessed. This determination is called the judgment.

In situations where the judgment is for monetary damages and the defendant does not voluntarily pay the set amount, the plaintiff can ask to have the court clerk issue an order to execute the judgment. The execution is issued to the sheriff and orders the sheriff to seize the defendant's property and sell it at auction to satisfy the judgment. An alternative is to order a lien, which is the legal right to hold property that may be used for the payment of the judgment.

Appeal. If one party feels that an error of law was made during the trial, and if the judge refuses to grant a posttrial motion for a new trial, then the dissatisfied party may appeal to a higher court. Probably the most common grounds for appeal are that the judge allegedly admitted evidence that should have been excluded, refused to admit evidence that should have been introduced, or failed to give proper jury instructions.

An attorney lays the groundwork for an appeal by objecting to the alleged error during the trial. This objection goes into the trial record and becomes a part of the trial transcript, which may be reviewed by an appellate court. The appellate court decision may call for the lower court to enforce its earlier verdict or to hold a new trial.   ⚖

FEDERAL
JUDGES

The movement to include minorities and women in the judiciary increased during the presidency of Jimmy Carter. President Ronald Reagan broke the gender barrier at the Supreme Court with his 1981 appointment of Sandra Day O'Connor, right, as Associate Justice. Chief Justice Warren Burger, left, is shown swearing her in, while her husband, John J. O'Connor, center, holds the two family Bibles.

The main actors in the federal system are the men and women who serve as judges and justices. What characteristics do these people have that distinguish them from the rest of the citizenry? What are the qualifications — both formal and informal — for appointment to the bench? How are judges selected and who are the participants in the process? How do judges learn to be judges? How are judges disciplined and when are they removed from the bench?

BACKGROUND CHARACTERISTICS OF FEDERAL JUDGES

Americans cling to the notion that someone born in the humblest of circumstances (such as Abraham Lincoln) may one day grow up to be the president of the United States, or at least a U.S. judge. As with most myths, this one has a kernel of truth. In principle virtually anyone can become a prominent public official, and a few well-known examples can be cited of people who came from poor backgrounds yet climbed to the pinnacle of power. More typically, however, America's federal judges, like other public officials and the captains of commerce and industry, come from the nation's middle and upper-middle classes.

District Judges

Background data for all federal district judges for the past 210 years have never been collected, but a good deal is known about judges who have served in recent decades.

Before assuming the federal bench, a plurality of judges had been judges at the state or local level. The next largest blocs were employed either in the political or governmental realms or in moderate- to large-sized law firms. Those working in small law firms or as professors of law made up the smallest bloc.

Judges' educational background reveals something of their elite nature. All graduated from college; about half attended either costly Ivy League schools or other private universities to receive their undergraduate and law degrees. Judges also differ from the population as a whole in that there is a strong tendency toward "occupational heredity" — that is, for judges to come from families with a tradition of judicial and public service.

Although the United States is about 51 percent female, judges have been almost exclusively male. Until the presidency of Jimmy Carter (1977-81), less than 2 percent of district judges were female, and even with conscious effort to change this phenomenon, only 14.4 percent of Carter's appointments to district judgeships were women. Racial minorities also have been underrepresented on the trial bench, not only in absolute numbers but also in comparison with figures for the overall population. Until the present time, only Jimmy Carter had appointed a significant number of non-Anglos to the federal bench — over 21 percent. During the administration of President Bill Clinton (1993-2001), a dramatic change took place. During his first six years in office, 49 percent of his judicial appointees were either women or minorities.

About nine out of ten district judges have been of the same political party as the appointing president, and historically about 60 percent have a record of active partisanship.

The typical judge has been 49 years old at the time of appointment. Age variations from one presidency to another have been small, with no discernible trend over the years from one administration to another.

Appeals Court Judges

Appeals judges are much more likely to have previous judicial experience than their counterparts on the trial court bench, and they are just as likely, if not more so, to have attended private and Ivy League schools.

In terms of political party affiliation, little difference is seen between trial and appellate court appointments. However, appeals judges have a slight tendency to be more active in their respective parties than their colleagues on the trial bench.

The Clinton initiative to make the bench more accurately reflect U.S. gender and racial demographics is evident in the ranks of the appellate judges as well. A third of his appointees were

women, and more African Americans, Hispanics, and Asians were appointed to the appellate court bench by Clinton than by any other president.

President George W. Bush, in turn, also has shown a commitment to racial and gender diversity. Almost one-third of his district court appointments, for example, have been "nontraditional" — women and minorities.

Supreme Court Justices

Since 1789, 106 men and two women have sat on the bench of America's highest judicial tribunal. Although perhaps 10 percent of the justices were essentially of humble origin, a majority of the justices came from politically active families, and about a third were related to jurists and closely connected with families with a tradition of judicial service.

Until the 1960s the High Court had been all white and all male, but in 1967 President Lyndon Johnson appointed Thurgood Marshall as the first African American member of the Court. When Marshall retired in 1991, President George H.W. Bush, father of President George W. Bush, replaced him with another African American, Clarence Thomas. In 1981 the gender barrier was broken when President Ronald Reagan named Sandra Day O'Connor to the Court, and 13 years later she was joined by Ruth Bader Ginsburg.

As for the nonpolitical occupations of the justices, all 108 had legal training and all had practiced law at some stage in their careers. Only 22 percent had state or federal judicial experience immediately prior to their appointments, although more than half had served on the bench at some time before their nomination to the Supreme Court. As with their colleagues in the lower federal judiciary, the justices were much more likely to have been politically active than the average American, and virtually all shared many of the ideological and political orientations of their appointing president.

QUALIFICATIONS OF FEDERAL JUDGES

Despite the absence of formal qualifications for a federal judgeship, there are well-defined informal requirements.

Formal Qualifications

No constitutional or statutory qualifications are stipulated for serving on the Supreme Court or the lower federal courts. The Constitution merely indicates that "the judicial Power of the United States, shall be vested in one supreme Court" as well as in any lower federal courts that Congress may establish (Article III, Section 1) and that the president "by and with the Advice and Consent of the Senate, shall appoint...Judges of the supreme Court" (Article II, Section 2). Congress has applied the same selection procedure to the appeals and the trial courts. There are no exams to pass, no minimum age requirement, no stipulation that judges be native-born citizens or legal residents, no requirement that judges even have a law degree.

Informal Requirements

At least four vital although informal factors determine who sits on the federal bench in America: professional competence, political qualifications, self-selection, and the element of luck.

Professional Competence: Although candidates for U.S. judicial posts do not have to be attorneys, it has been the custom to appoint lawyers who have distinguished themselves professionally. Although the political rules may allow a president to reward an old ally with a seat on the bench, tradition has created an expectation that the would-be judge have some reputation for professional competence, the more so as the judgeship in question goes from the trial court to the appeals court to the Supreme Court level.

Political Qualifications: Most nominees for judicial office have some record of political activity for two reasons. First, to some degree judgeships are still considered part of the political patronage system; those who have served the party are more likely to be rewarded with a federal post than those who have not. Second, some political activity on the part of the would-be judge is often necessary, because otherwise the candidate would simply not be visible to the president, senator(s), or local party leaders who send forth the names of candidates.

Self-Selection: While many consider it undignified and lacking in judicial temperament for someone to announce publicly a desire for a federal judgeship, some would-be jurists orchestrate discreet campaigns on their own behalf or at least pass the word that they are available for judicial service. Few will admit to seeking an appointment actively, but credible anecdotes suggest that attorneys often position themselves in such a way that their names will come up when there is a vacant seat to fill.

The Element of Luck: A good measure of happenstance exists in virtually all judicial appointments. Being a member of the right party at the right time or being visible to the power brokers at the right moment often has as much to do with becoming a judge as one's professional background.

THE FEDERAL SELECTION PROCESS AND ITS PARTICIPANTS

The framework of judicial selection is the same for all federal judges, although the roles of the participants vary depending on the level of the U.S. judiciary. All nominations are made by the president after due consultation with the White House staff, the attorney general's office, certain senators, and other politi-cal operatives. The Federal Bureau of Investigation (FBI), an arm of the Justice Department, customarily performs a routine security check. After the nomination is announced to the public, various interest groups that believe they have a stake in the appointment may lobby for or against the candidate. Also, the candidate's qualifications will be evaluated by a committee of the American Bar Association. The candidate's name is sent to the Senate Judiciary Committee, which conducts an investigation of the nominee's fitness for the post. If the committee's vote is favorable, the nomination is sent to the floor of the Senate, where it is either approved or rejected by a simple majority vote.

The President

Technically, the president nominates all judicial candidates, but historically the chief executive has been more involved in appointments to the Supreme Court than to the lower courts. This is so for two major reasons.

First, Supreme Court appointments are seen by the president — and by the public at large — as generally more important and politically significant than openings on the lesser tribunals. Presidents often use their few opportunities for High Court appointments to make a political statement or to set the tone of their administration. For example, during the period of national stress prior to U.S. entry into World War II, Democratic President Franklin D. Roosevelt elevated Republican Harlan Fiske Stone to chief justice as a gesture of national unity. In 1969 President Richard Nixon used his appointment of the conservative Warren Burger to fulfill his campaign pledge to restore "law and order." And President Ronald Reagan in 1981 hoped to dispel his reputation for being unsympathetic toward the women's movement by being the first to name a woman to the High Court.

A second reason why presidents are likely to devote more attention to Supreme Court appointments and less to lower court appointments is that tradition has allowed for individual senators and local party leaders to influence, and often dominate, lower court appointments. The practice known as senatorial courtesy is part of the appointment process for district judges. Under senatorial courtesy, senators of the president's political party who are from the home state of the nominee are asked their opinions of the candidate by the Senate Judiciary Committee. In expressing their views about a particular candidate, these senators are in a position to virtually veto a nomination. Senatorial courtesy does not apply to appellate court appointments, although it is customary for presidents to defer to senators of their party from states that make up the appellate court circuit.

The Department of Justice

Assisting the president and the White House staff in the judicial selection process are the two key presidential appointees in the Justice Department — the attorney general of the United

President Lyndon B. Johnson, right, appointed the first African American member of the Supreme Court, Thurgood Marshall, left, in 1967.

States and the deputy attorney general. Their primary job is to seek out candidates for federal judicial posts who conform to general criteria set by the president. Once several names are obtained, the staff of the Justice Department will subject each candidate to further scrutiny. They may order an FBI investigation of the candidate's character and background; they will usually read copies of all articles or speeches the candidate has written or evaluate a sitting judge's written opinions; they might check with local party leaders to determine that the candidate is a party faithful and is in tune with the president's major public policy positions.

In the case of district judge appointments, where names are often submitted by home-state senators, the Justice Department's function is more that of screener than of initiator. Regardless of who comes up with a list of names, the Justice Department's primary duty is to evaluate the candidate's personal, professional, and political qualifications. In performing this role the department may work closely with the White House staff, with the senators involved in the nomination, and with party leaders who may wish to have some input in choosing the nominee.

State and Local Party Leaders

Regional party leaders have little to say in the appointment of Supreme Court justices, where presidential prerogative is dominant, and their role in the choice of appeals court judges is minimal. However, in the selection of U.S. trial judges their impact is formidable, especially when appointments occur in states in which neither senator is of the president's political party. In such cases the president will be more likely to consult with state leaders of his own party rather than with the state's senators.

Interest Groups

A number of pressure groups in the United States, representing the whole political spectrum from left to right, often lobby either for or against judicial nominations. Leaders of these groups — civil liberties, business, organized labor, civil rights — have little hesitation about urging the president to withdraw the nomination of someone whose political and social values are different from their own or about lobbying the Senate to support the nomination of someone who is favorably perceived. Interest groups lobby for and against nominees at all levels of the federal judiciary.

The American Bar Association (ABA)

For more than five decades, the Committee on the Federal Judiciary of the ABA has played a key role in evaluating the professional credentials of potential nominees for positions on the federal bench. The committee, whose 15 members represent all the

The President nominates all federal judicial candidates, but individual senators and local party leaders traditionally wield a lot of influence in the case of lower court appointments. Above, two U.S. district court judges presiding in a naturalization ceremony in New York State. Center, President George W. Bush congratulates his nominees to federal judgeships. Bottom, Senior Judge Constance Baker Motley, right, of the U.S. District Court for the Southern District of New York speaks at a panel discussion.

U.S. circuits, evaluates candidates on the basis of three criteria: judicial temperament, professional competence, and integrity. A candidate approved by the committee is rated either "qualified" or "well qualified," whereas an unacceptable candidate is stamped with a "not qualified" label.

The Senate Judiciary Committee

The rules of the Senate require its Judiciary Committee to consider all nominations to the federal bench and to make recommendations to the Senate as a whole. Its role is thus to screen individuals who have already been nominated, not to suggest names of possible candidates. The committee holds hearings on all nominations, at which time witnesses are heard and deliberations take place behind closed doors. The hearings for district court appointments are largely perfunctory because the norm of senatorial courtesy has, for all intents and purposes, already determined whether the candidate will be acceptable to the Senate. However, for appeals court nominees — and surely for an appointment to the Supreme Court — the committee hearing is a serious proceeding.

The Senate

The final step in the judicial appointment process for federal judges is a majority vote by the Senate. Historically, two general views have prevailed of the Senate's prescribed role. Presidents from the time of George Washington and a few scholars have taken the position that the Senate ought quietly to go along with the presidential choices unless overwhelmingly strong reasons exist to the contrary. Other scholars and most senators have held the view that the Senate has the right and the obligation to make its own decision regarding the nominee. In practice the role of the Senate in the judicial confirmation process has varied, depending on the level of the federal judgeship that is being considered.

For district judges the norm of senatorial courtesy prevails. That is, if the president's nominee is acceptable to the senator(s) of the president's party in the state in which the judge is to sit, the Senate is usually happy to confirm the appointment. For appointments to the appeals courts, senatorial courtesy does not apply, since the vacancy to be filled covers more than just the state of one or possibly two senators. But senators from each state in the circuit in which the vacancy has occurred customarily submit names of possible candidates to the president. An unwritten rule is that each state in the circuit should have at least one judge on that circuit's appellate bench. As long as the norms are adhered to and the president's nominee has reasonably good qualifications, the Senate as a whole usually goes along with the recommendations of the chief executive.

The Senate has been inclined to dispute the president if disagreement arises over a nominee's fitness for the

High Court. Since 1789, presidents have sent the names of 144 Supreme Court nominees to the Senate for its advice and consent. Of this number, 30 were either rejected or "indefinitely postponed" by the Senate, or the names were withdrawn by the president. Thus presidents have been successful about 79 percent of the time, and their success rate seems to be improving, given that as many as one-third of the nominations were rejected by the Senate in the 19th century. The record shows that presidents have met with the most success in getting their High Court nominations approved when the nominee comes from a non-controversial background and has middle-of-the-road political leanings, and when the president's party also controls the Senate, or at least a majority shares the president's basic attitudes and values.

THE JUDICIAL SOCIALIZATION PROCESS

In college and law school, future judges acquire important analytic and communication skills, in addition to the basic substance of the law. After a couple of decades of legal practice, the future judge has learned a good bit about how the courts and the law actually work and has specialized in several areas of the law. Despite all this preparation, sometimes called "anticipatory socialization," most new judges in America still have a lot to learn about being a judge.

Not only does the United States lack formalized training procedures for the judicial profession, but there is an assumption that being a lawyer for a decade or so is all the experience one needs to be a judge. On the contrary, becoming a judge in America requires a good deal of freshman socialization (short-term learning and adjustment to the new role) and occupational socialization (on-the-job training over a period of years).

Typical new trial court appointees may be first-rate lawyers and experts in a few areas of the law in which they have specialized. As judges, however, they are expected to be experts on all legal subjects, are required to engage in judicial duties usually unrelated to any tasks they performed as lawyers (for example, sentencing), and are given a host of administrative assignments for which they have had no prior experience (for example, learning how to docket efficiently several hundred diverse cases).

At the appeals court level there is also a period of freshman socialization — despite the circuit judge's possible prior judicial experience — and former trial judges appear to make the transition more easily. During the transition time, circuit judges tend to speak less for the court than their more experienced colleagues. They often take longer to write opinions, defer more often to senior colleagues, or experience a period of indecision.

The learning process for new Supreme Court justices is even harder. As with new appeals court judges, novice Supreme Court justices tend to defer to senior associates, to write fewer majority and dissenting opinions, and to manifest a degree of uncertainty. New High Court appointees may have more judicial experience than their lower-court colleagues, but the fact that the Supreme Court is involved in broad judicial policy making — as opposed to the error correction of the appeals courts and the norm enforcement of the trial courts — may account for their initial indecisiveness.

Given the need on the part of all new federal jurists for both freshman and occupational socialization, where do they go for instruction? For both the appeals court judges and their trial court peers, most of their training comes from their more senior, experienced colleagues on the bench — particularly the chief judge of the circuit or district. Likewise on the Supreme Court, older associates, often the chief justice, play a primary part in passing on to novice justices the essential rules and values of the Court.

Training seminars provided by the Federal Judicial Center for newly appointed judges also play an important role in the training and socialization of new jurists. Although some of these seminars are conducted by outsider specialists — subject matter experts in the law schools — the key instructors tend to be seasoned judges whose real-life experience on the bench commands the respect of the new members of the federal judiciary.

What is the significance of this socialization process for the operation of the U.S. judicial-legal system? First, the agents of socialization that are readily available to the novice jurists allow the system to operate more smoothly, with a minimum of down time. If new judges were isolated from their more experienced associates, geographically or otherwise, they would require more time to learn the fine points of their trade and presumably a greater number of errors would occur in litigation.

Second, the fact that the system is able to provide its own socialization — that the older, experienced jurists train the novices — serves as a sort of glue that helps bond the system together. It allows the judicial values, practices, and orientations of one generation of judges to be passed on to another. It gives continuity and a sense of permanence to a system that operates in a world where chaos and random behavior are common.

THE RETIREMENT AND REMOVAL OF JUDGES

Judges cease performing their judicial duties when they retire by choice or because of ill health or death, or when they are subjected to the disciplinary actions of others.

Disciplinary Action Against Federal Judges

All federal judges appointed under the provisions of Article III of the Constitution hold office "during good Behavior," which means in effect for life or until they choose to step down. The only way they can be removed from the bench is by impeachment (indictment by the House of Representatives) and conviction by the Senate. In accordance with constitutional requirements (for Supreme Court justices) and legislative standards (for appeals and trial court judges), impeachment may occur for "Treason, Bribery, or other high Crimes and Misdemeanors." An impeached jurist would face trial in the Senate, which could convict by a vote of two-thirds of the members present.

Since 1789 the House of Representatives has initiated impeachment proceedings against only 13 jurists — although about an equal number of judges resigned just before formal action was taken against them. Of these 13 cases, only seven resulted in a conviction, which removed them from office.

Although outright acts of criminality by those on the bench are few, a gray area of misconduct may put offending judges somewhere between acceptable and impeachable behavior. What to do with the federal jurist who hears a case despite an obvious conflict of interest, who consistently demonstrates biased behavior in the courtroom, whose personal habits negatively affect his or her performance in court? Historically, little has been done in such cases other than issuance of a mild reprimand by colleagues. In recent decades, however, actions have been taken to discipline judges.

On October 1, 1980, a new statute of Congress took effect. Titled the Judicial Councils Reform and Judicial Conduct and Disability Act, the law has two distinct parts. The first part authorizes the Judicial Council in each circuit, composed of both appeals and trial court judges and presided over by the chief judge of the circuit, to "make all necessary and appropriate orders for the effective and expeditious administration of justice within its circuit." The second part of the act establishes a statutory complaint procedure against judges. Briefly, it permits an aggrieved party to file a written complaint with the clerk of the appellate court. The chief judge then reviews the charge and may dismiss it if it appears frivolous, or for a variety of other reasons. If the complaint seems valid, the chief judge must appoint an investigating committee consisting of himself or herself and an equal number of trial and circuit court judges. After an inquiry the committee reports to the council, which has several options: the judge may be exonerated; if the offender is a bankruptcy judge or magistrate, he or she may be removed; and an Article III judge may be subject to private or public reprimand or censure, certification of disability, request for voluntary resignation, or prohibition against further case assignments. However, removal of an Article III judge is not permitted; impeachment is still the only recourse. If the council determines that the conduct might constitute grounds for impeachment, it will notify the Judicial Conference, which in turn may transmit the case to the U.S. House of Representatives for consideration.

Disability of Federal Judges

Perhaps more problematic than removing jurists for misconduct is the removal of those who have become too old and infirm to carry out their judicial responsibilities effectively. Congress has tried with some success to tempt the more senior judges into retirement by making it financially more attractive to do so. Since 1984 federal judges have been permitted to retire with full pay and benefits under what is called the rule of 80; that is, when the sum of a judge's age and number of years on the bench is 80. Congress has also permitted judges to go on senior status instead of accepting full retirement. In exchange for a reduced caseload they are permitted to retain their office and staff and — equally important — the prestige and self-respect of being an active judge.

Judges often time their resignations to occur when their party controls the presidency so that they will be replaced by a jurist of similar political and judicial orientation. A 1990 study found that especially since 1954, "judicial retirement/resignation rates have been strongly influenced by political/ideological considerations, and infused with partisanship," thus indicating that many jurists view themselves as part of a policy link between the people, the judicial appointment process, and the subsequent decisions of the judges and justices. ⚖

QUALIFICATIONS AND BACKGROUNDS OF STATE JUDGES

Most state laws and constitutions provide few rigid conditions for being a state judge. The vast majority of the states do not require their justices of the peace or magistrates to have law degrees, but such degrees are virtually required (either formally or in practice) for trial and appellate judges.

Although women constitute a slight majority of the American population and despite the upsurge in recent decades in the number of women in the legal profession, women are still underrepresented on the bench. Those who do serve as state jurists are much more likely to serve at the lower levels of the state judiciary than on the supreme courts, although this varies greatly from one state to the next. As of the mid-1990s, only about 14 percent of all state judges were women and 6 percent were either African American, Hispanic, or Asian American.

State judges, like their federal counterparts, have generally stayed in the region where they grew up and were educated. About three-fourths of all state jurists were born in the state in which they serve, and less than a third went out of state for their undergraduate degrees or for their law degrees. This penchant for localism is also reflected in the patterns of work experience that state judges bring to the bench. For example, of those serving on the state supreme court bench, only 13 percent have any prior federal experience, whereas 93 percent have some type of prior state experience.

Judges tend to be middle-aged when they assume the bench. State trial judges come to the bench at about age 46, which corresponds roughly to the figure of 49 for federal trial judges. State appellate court judges tend to be slightly older than their trial court colleagues when they become jurists — about 53, which is approximately the same as their federal equivalents.

In terms of political party affiliation, state judges, whether they be elected or appointed, tend to mirror the party that dominates in the judge's state. Also, the vast majority of state judges had been politically active before assuming the bench, whether they were elected to the bench or appointed by a governor.

Over half the state trial judges come to the bench from the private practice of law, and about a quarter were elevated from a lower court judgeship, such as a magistrate's position. Of those who practiced law, most reported a general practice without specialization. About one in five was recruited from the ranks of

district attorneys, and only 3 percent come from private criminal law practice. Of those serving on state supreme courts, almost two-thirds came from the ranks of the intermediate appellate courts or from the state trial courts.

THE SELECTION PROCESS FOR STATE JUDGES

At the state level a variety of methods are used to select jurists, and each of these has many permutations. Basically, there are five routes to a judgeship in any one of the 50 states: partisan election, nonpartisan election, merit selection, gubernatorial appointment, and appointment by the legislature.

Election of Judges

The election of judges, on either a partisan or a nonpartisan ballot, is the norm in the states. This method became popular during the time of President Andrew Jackson (1829-37), an era when Americans sought to democratize the political process. In practice, however, political party leaders often regard judicial elections as indirect patronage to reward the party faithful. Also, judges who must run for election are often forced to solicit campaign contributions from the lawyers and law firms that will eventually appear before them in court — a potential source of conflict of interest. Finally, voter turnout in judicial elections is extremely low. Voters may know whom they prefer for president or member of Congress or state senator, but they may be unfamiliar with the persons running for state judgeships.

As part of the Progressive movement at the turn of the 20th century, reformers sought to take some of the partisanship out of judicial elections by having judges run on a nonpartisan basis. In principle they would run on their ideas and qualifications, not on the basis of which party they belonged to. But even in these technically nonpartisan states, the political parties endorse individual judicial candidates and contribute to their campaigns so that the candidates acquire identification with one political party or another.

Merit Selection

Merit selection has been in use since the early 1900s as a preferred method of selecting judges. The first state fully to adopt such a method

was Missouri in 1940, and ever since such schemes have come to be known as generic variants of "the Missouri Plan."

The states with Missouri-type plans use a combination of elections and appointments. The governor appoints a judge from among several candidates recommended by a nominating panel of five or more people, usually including attorneys (often chosen by the local bar association), nonlawyers appointed by the governor, and sometimes a senior local judge. Either by law or by implicit agreement, the governor appoints someone from the recommended list. After serving for a short period of time, often a year, the newly appointed judge must stand for a special election, at which time he or she in effect runs on his or her record. (The voters are asked, "Shall Judge X be retained in office?") If the judge's tenure is supported by the voters, as is virtually always the case, the judge will serve for a regular and fairly long term.

Gubernatorial Appointment and Legislative Appointment

Today, judges are chosen by the governor or by the state legislature in only a handful of states. When judges are appointed by the governor, politics almost invariably comes into play. Governors tend to select individuals who have been active in state politics and whose activity has benefited either the governor personally or the governor's political party or allies. Also, in making judicial appointments the governor often bargains with local political leaders or with state legislators whose support he or she needs. A governor may also use a judgeship to reward a legislator or local politician who has given faithful political support in the past.

Only a few states still allow their legislators to appoint state judges. Although a variety of criteria may be used in choosing members of the state supreme courts, when it comes to filling the state trial benches, state legislators tend to turn to former members of the legislature.

THE RETIREMENT AND REMOVAL OF JUDGES

Judges who are too old or unfit to serve seem to be less of a problem at the state level than at the federal level. A number of states have mandatory retirement plans. Minimum ages for retirement range from 65 to 75, with 70 being the most common. Some states have declining retirement benefit plans for judges who serve beyond the desired tenure; that is, the longer judges stay on the bench, the lower their retirement benefits.

Retirement plans, no matter how effective in getting the older judge to resign, are of little use against the younger jurist who is incompetent, corrupt, or unethical. Throughout American history the states have used procedures such as impeachment, recall elections, and concurrent resolutions of the legislature to dismiss these judges. These methods were only minimally effective, however, either because they proved to be politically difficult to put into operation or because of their time-consuming, cumbersome nature.

More recently, the states have begun to set up special commissions, often made up of the judges themselves, to police their own members. Such commissions are not always effective, however, because judges are often loath to expose a colleague to public censure and discipline.

IMPLEMENTATION
AND
IMPACT
OF
JUDICIAL
POLICIES

A prosecuting attorney argues before
the Washington State Supreme Court,
one of the lower courts normally seen
as the enforcers of the policies made
by rulings by appellate courts, notably
the U.S. Supreme Court.

After a court's decision is reached, a variety of individuals — other judges, public officials, even private citizens — may be called upon to implement the decision. This chapter looks at the various actors involved in the implementation process, their reactions to judicial policies, and the methods by which they may respond to a court's decision.

Depending upon the nature of the court's ruling, the judicial policy may have a very narrow or a very broad impact. A suit for damages incurred in an automobile accident would directly affect only the persons involved and perhaps their immediate families. But the famous *Gideon v. Wainwright* (1963) decision has directly affected millions of people in one way or another. In *Gideon* the Supreme Court held that states must provide an attorney for indigent defendants in felony trials. Scores of people — defendants, judges, lawyers, taxpayers — have felt the effects of that judicial policy.

THE IMPACT OF HIGHER-COURT DECISIONS ON LOWER COURTS

Appellate courts, notably the U.S. Supreme Court, often are viewed as the most likely courts to be involved in policy making, while the trial courts are generally seen as norm enforcers. However, lower-court judges have a great deal of independence from the appellate courts and may be viewed, according to one study, as "independent actors...who will not follow the lead of higher courts unless conditions are favorable for their doing so."

Lower-Court Discretion

Why do the lower-court judges have so much discretion when it comes to implementing a higher court's policy? In part, the answer may be found in the structure of the U.S. judicial system. The judiciary has always been characterized by independence, decentralization, and individualism. Federal judges, for example, are protected by life tenure and traditionally have been able to run their courts as they see fit. Disciplinary measures are not at all common, and federal judges have historically had little fear of impeachment. To retain their positions, the state trial court judges generally have only to keep the electorate satisfied.

The discretion exercised by a lower-court judge may also be a product of the higher court's decision itself. For example, following the famous school desegregation case, *Brown v. Board of Education of Topeka* (1954), the Supreme Court told federal district judges, who had the task of enforcing the ruling, that the public schools were to make a prompt and reasonable start and then proceed with all deliberate speed to bring about desegregation. What constitutes a prompt and reasonable start? How rapidly must a school district proceed in order to be moving with all deliberate speed?

The Supreme Court did not provide specific answers to these questions.

Although not all High Court decisions are so open to interpretation, a good number of them are. A court's decision may be unclear for several reasons. Sometimes the issue or subject matter may be so complex that it is difficult to fashion a clear policy. In obscenity cases, for instance, the Supreme Court has had little difficulty in deciding that pornographic material is not entitled to protection as free speech under the First Amendment to the Constitution. Defining obscenity has proven to be another matter, however. Phrases such as "prurient interest," "patently offensive," "contemporary community standards," and "without redeeming social value" have become commonplace in obscenity opinions, but these terms leave a good deal of room for subjective interpretation.

Policies established by collegial courts are often ambiguous because the majority opinion is written to accommodate several judges. The majority opinion may also be accompanied by several concurring opinions. When this happens, lower court judges are left without a clear-cut precedent to follow. For example, in *Furman v. Georgia* (1972), the Supreme Court struck down the death penalty in several states, but for a variety of reasons. Some justices opposed the death penalty per se, on the ground that it constituted cruel and unusual punishment in violation of the Eighth Amendment to the Constitution. Others voted to strike down the state laws because they were applied in a discriminatory manner. The uncertainty created by the 1972 decision affected not only lower-court judges but also state legislatures. The states passed a rash of widely divergent death penalty statutes and caused a considerable amount of new litigation.

A lower-court judge's discretion in the implementation process may also be affected by the manner in which a higher court's policy is communicated. Certainly the court from which a case has been appealed will be informed of the decision. However, systematic, formal efforts are not made to inform other courts of the decision or to see that lower-court judges have access to a copy of the opinion. The decisions that contain the new judicial policy are made available to the public in printed form or on the Internet, and judges are expected to read them if they have the time and inclination.

Opinions of the Supreme Court, lower federal courts, and state appellate courts are available in a large number of courthouse, law school, and university libraries. They are also increasingly available on the Internet. This widespread availability does not guarantee that they will be read and clearly understood, however. Many lower-level state judges, such as justices of the peace and juvenile court judges, are nonlawyers who have little interest or skill in reading complex judicial decisions. Finally, even those judges who have an interest in higher-court decisions and the ability to understand them do not have adequate time to keep abreast of all the new opinions.

Given these problems, how do judges become aware of upper-court decisions? One way is to hear of them through lawyers presenting cases in the lower courts. It is generally assumed that the opposing attorneys will present relevant precedents in their arguments before the judge. Those judges who have law clerks may also rely upon them to search out recent decisions from higher courts.

Thus some higher-court policies are not quickly and strictly enforced simply because lower-court judges are not aware of them. Even those policies which lower-court judges are aware of may not be so clear to them. Either reason contributes to the discretion exercised by lower-court judges placed in the position of having to implement judicial policies.

Interpretation by Lower Courts

One study noted that "important policy announcements almost always require interpretation by someone other than the policy maker." This is certainly true in the case of judicial policies established by appellate courts. The first exercise of a lower-court judge's discretion may be to interpret what the higher court's decision means.

The manner in which a lower-court judge interprets a policy established by a higher court depends upon a number of factors. Many policies are not clearly stated. Thus reasonable people may disagree over the proper interpretation. Even policy pronouncements that do not suffer from ambiguity, however, are sometimes interpreted differently by different judges.

A judge's own personal policy preferences will also have an effect upon the interpretation he or she gives to a higher-court policy. Judges come to the courts with their own unique background characteristics. Some are Republican, others are Democrat; one judge may be more lenient, another strict. They come from different regions of the country. Some have been prosecutors; others have been primarily defense lawyers or corporate lawyers. In short, their backgrounds may influence their own particular policy preferences. Thus the lower-court judges may read their own ideas into a higher-court policy. The result is that a policy may be enthusiastically embraced by some judges yet totally rejected by others.

Strategies Employed by Lower Courts

Judges who favor and accept a higher court's policy will naturally try to enforce it and perhaps even expand upon it. Some judges even have risked social ostracism and various kinds of harassment in order to implement policies they believed in but that were not popular in their communities.

Judges who do not like a higher court's policy decision may implement it sparingly or only under duress. A judge who basically disagrees with a policy established by a higher court can employ a number of strategies. One rarely used strategy is defiance, whereby a judge simply does not apply the higher court's policy in a case before a lower court.

Such outright defiance is highly unusual. Other strategies are not so extreme. One is simply to avoid having to apply the policy. A case may be disposed of on technical or procedural grounds so that the judge does not have to rule on the actual merits of the case. It may be determined, for example, that the plaintiff does not have standing to sue or that the case has become moot because the issue was resolved before the trial commenced. Lower-court judges sometimes avoid accepting a policy by declaring a portion of the higher-court decision to be "dicta" (Latin, meaning an authoritative declaration). Dicta refers to the part of the opinion that does not contribute to the central logic of the decision. It may be useful as guidance but is not seen as binding. What constitutes dicta is open to varying interpretations.

Another strategy used by judges who are in basic disagreement with a judicial policy is to apply it as narrowly as possible. One method is for the lower-court judge to rule that a precedent is not controlling because factual differences exist between the higher-court case and the case before the lower courts. That is, because the two cases may be distinguished, the precedent does not have to be followed.

Influences on Lower-Court Judges

At times the lower courts must decide cases for which no precise standards have been provided by the higher courts. Whenever this occurs, lower-court judges must turn elsewhere for guidance in deciding a case before them. One study notes that lower-court judges in such a position "may take their cues on how to decide a particular case from a wide variety of factors including their party affiliation, their ideology, or their regional norms."

CONGRESSIONAL INFLUENCES ON THE IMPLEMENTATION PROCESS

Once a federal judicial decision is made, Congress can offer a variety of responses: It may aid or hinder the implementation of a decision. In addition, it can alter a court's interpretation of the law. Finally, Congress can mount an attack on an individual judge.

In the course of deciding cases, the courts are often called upon to interpret federal statutes. On occasion the judicial interpretation may differ from what a majority in Congress intended. When that situation occurs, Congress can change the statute in new legislation that in effect overrules the court's initial interpretation. However, the vast majority of the federal judiciary's statutory decisions are not changed by Congress.

Besides ruling on statutes, the federal courts interpret the Constitution. Congress has two methods to reverse or alter the effects of a constitutional interpretation it does not like. First, Congress can respond with another statute designed to avoid the constitutional problems. Second, a constitutional decision can be overturned directly by an amendment to the U.S. Constitution. Although many such amendments have been intro-

President Lyndon B. Johnson, after signing into law the Civil Rights Act of 1964, reaches to shake hands with Dr. Martin Luther King, Jr. This law was an example of Congress' key role in implementing a decision by the Supreme Court, in this instance, school desegregation policy.

duced over the years, it is not easy to obtain the necessary two-thirds vote in each house of Congress to propose the amendment and then achieve ratification by three-fourths of the states. Only four Supreme Court decisions in the history of the Court have been overturned by constitutional amendments.

Congressional attacks on the federal courts in general and on certain judges in particular are another method of responding to judicial decisions. These attacks may take the form of verbal denouncements by a member of Congress, threats of impeachment of sitting judges, or more thorough investigations of the judicial philosophies of potential nominees to the federal bench.

Congress and the federal courts are not natural adversaries, however. Retaliations against the federal judiciary are fairly rare, and often the two branches work in harmony toward similar policy goals. For example, Congress played a key role in implementing the Supreme Court's school desegregation policy by enacting the Civil Rights Act of 1964, which empowered the Justice Department to initiate suits against school districts that failed to comply with the *Brown v. Board of Education* decision. Title VI of the Act also provided a potent weapon in the desegregation struggle by threatening the denial of federal funds to schools guilty of segregation. In 1965 Congress further solidified its

support for a policy of desegregated public schools by passing the Elementary and Secondary Education Act. This act gave the federal government a much larger role in financing public education and thus made the threat to cut off federal funds a serious problem for many segregated school districts. Such support from Congress was significant because the likelihood of compliance with a policy is increased when there is unity between branches of government.

EXECUTIVE BRANCH INFLUENCES ON THE IMPLEMENTATION PROCESS

At times the president may be called upon directly to implement a judicial decision. An example is *United States v. Nixon* (1974). A Senate committee investigation into the cover-up of a break-in at the Democratic Party headquarters in the Watergate Hotel in Washington, D.C., led directly to high government officials working close to the president. It was also revealed during the investigation that President Richard Nixon had installed an automatic taping system in the Oval Office. Leon Jaworski, who had been appointed special prosecutor to investigate the Watergate affair, subpoenaed certain tapes that he felt might provide evidence needed in his prosecution of high-ranking officials. Nixon refused to turn over the tapes on grounds of executive privilege and the need for confidentiality in discussions leading to presidential decisions. The Supreme Court's decision instructed the president to surrender the subpoenaed tapes to Judge John J. Sirica, who was handling the trials of the government officials. Nixon did comply with the High Court's directive and thus a decision was implemented that quickly led to his downfall. Within two weeks he resigned from the presidency, in August 1974.

Even when not directly involved in the enforcement of a judicial policy, the president may be able to influence its impact. Because of the status and visibility of the position, a president, simply by words and actions, may encourage support for, or resistance to, a new judicial policy.

A president can propose legislation that directly affects the courts. President Franklin D. Roosevelt, for instance, unsuccessfully urged Congress to increase the size of the Supreme Court so he could "pack" it with justices who supported his administration's legislative agenda.

The appointment power also gives the president an opportunity to influence federal judicial policies, as the president appoints all federal judges, with the advice and consent of the Senate.

A president can influence judicial policy making through the activities of the Justice Department, a part of the executive branch. The attorney general and staff subordinates can empha-size specific issues according to the overall policy goals of the president. The other side of the coin, however, is that the Justice Department may, at its discretion, de-emphasize specific policies by not pursuing them vigorously in the courts.

Another official who is in a position to influence judicial policy making is the solicitor general. Historically, this official has been seen as having dual responsibility to both the judicial and executive branches. Because of the solicitor general's close relationship with the Supreme Court, this official is sometimes referred to as the "tenth justice." The solicitor general is often seen as a counselor who advises the Court about the meaning of federal statutes and the Constitution. The solicitor general also determines which of the cases involving the federal government as a party will be appealed to the Supreme Court. Furthermore, he or she may file an amicus curiae brief urging the Court to grant or deny another litigant's certiorari petition or supporting or opposing a particular policy being urged upon the High Court.

Many judicial decisions are actually implemented by the various departments, agencies, bureaus, and commissions of the executive branch. For example, the Supreme Court decision in *Frontiero v. Richardson* (1973) called upon the U.S. Air Force to play the major implementation role. The *Frontiero* case questioned congressional statutes that provided benefits for married male members of the Air Force but did not provide similar benefits for married female members. Lieutenant Sharron Frontiero challenged the policy on the ground that it constituted sexual discrimination. A federal district court in Alabama issued a decision upholding the Air Force policy. Lieutenant Frontiero appealed to the Supreme Court, which overturned the lower court decision and required the Air Force to implement a new policy.

OTHER IMPLEMENTERS

The implementation of judicial policies is often performed by state as well as federal officials. Many of the Supreme Court's criminal due process decisions, such as *Gideon v. Wainwright* and *Miranda v. Arizona* (1966), have been enforced by state court judges and other state officials. State and local police officers, for instance, have played a major role in implementing the *Miranda* requirement that criminal suspects must be advised of their rights. The *Gideon* ruling that an attorney must be provided at state expense for indigent defendants in felony trials has been implemented by public defenders, local bar associations, and individual court-appointed lawyers.

State legislators and executives are also frequently drawn into the implementation process. A judge who determines that a wrong has been committed may choose from a variety of options to remedy the wrong. Among the more common options are process remedies, performance standards, and specified remedial actions. Process remedies provide for such things as advisory committees, citizen participation, educational programs, evaluation committees, dispute resolution procedures, and special masters to address a problem and come up with a solution. The remedies do not specify a particular form of action. Performance standards call for specific remedies — for example, a certain number of housing units or schools or a certain level of staffing in a prison or mental health facility. The specific means of attaining these goals are left to the discretion of the officials named in the suit. Examples of specified remedial actions are school busing, altered school attendance zones, and changes in the size and condition of prison cells or hospital rooms. This type of remedy provides the defendant with no flexibility concerning the specific remedy or the means of attaining it.

Implementation of these remedial decrees often devolves, at least partially, to the state legislatures. An order calling for a certain number of prison cells or a certain number of guards in the prison system might require new state expenditures, which the legislature would have to fund. Similarly, an order to construct more modern mental health facilities or provide more modern equipment would mean an increase in state expenditures. Governors would also be involved in carrying out these types of remedial decrees because they typically are heavily involved in state budgeting procedures. Also, they may sign or veto laws.

Sometimes judges appoint certain individuals to assist in carrying out the remedial decree. Special masters are usually given some decision-making authority. Court-appointed monitors are also used in some situations, but they do not relieve the judge of decision-making responsibilities. Instead, the monitor is an information gatherer who reports on the defendant's progress in complying with the remedial decree. When orders are not implemented or when barriers of one kind or another block progress in providing a remedy, a judge may name someone as a receiver and empower him or her to disregard normal organizational barriers to get the job done.

One group of individuals has been deeply involved in implementing judicial policies: the thousands of men and women who constitute school boards throughout the country. Two major policy areas stand out as having embroiled school board members in considerable controversy as they faced the task of trying to carry out Supreme Court policy.

First, when the High Court ruled in 1954 that segregation has no place in the public schools, school boards and school superintendents, along with federal district judges, bore the brunt of implementing that decision. Their role in this process has affected the lives of millions of schoolchildren, parents, and taxpayers all over America.

The second area that has involved school boards is the Supreme Court's policies on religion in the public schools. In *Engel v. Vitale* (1962), the Court held unconstitutional a New York requirement that a state-written prayer be recited daily in the public schools. Some school districts responded to the decision by requiring instead the recitation of a Bible verse or the Lord's Prayer. Their reasoning was that since the state did not write the Lord's Prayer or the Bible, they were not violating the Court's policy. A year later, the Supreme Court struck down these new practices, pointing out that the constitutional violation lay in endorsing the religious activity and its determination did not depend on whether the state had written the prayer.

THE IMPACT OF JUDICIAL POLICIES

The ultimate importance of the Supreme Court's decisions depends primarily on their impact on American society as a whole. A few policies that have had significant effects are in the areas of racial equality, criminal due process, and abortion.

Racial Equality

Many point to the Supreme Court's decision in *Brown v. Board of Education* as the impetus for the drive for racial equality in the United States. However, Congress and the executive branch were also involved in the process of ensuring implementation of the decision's desegregation policy. Still, the courts initiated the pursuit for a national policy of racial equality with the *Brown* ruling.

In the beginning, the court decisions were often vague, leading to evasion of the new policy. The Supreme Court justices and many lower federal judges were persistent, however, and kept the policy of racial equality on the national political agenda. Their persistence paid off with passage of the 1964 Civil Rights Act, 10 years after the *Brown* decision. That act, which had the strong support of Presidents John F. Kennedy (1961-63) and Lyndon B. Johnson (1963-69), squarely placed Congress and the president on record as being supportive of racial equality in America.

One other aspect of the federal judiciary's importance in the policymaking process is illustrated by the *Brown* decision and the cases that followed it. Although the courts stood virtually alone in the quest for racial equality for several years, their decisions did not go unnoticed. Charles A.

Virginia Military Institute cadets say grace before their evening meal of April 2, 2001, shortly after the American Civil Liberties Union filed suit to force the school to drop the prayers. The role of religion in public schools has been one of the most disputed issues before the U.S. court system in the past 40 years.

Johnson and Bradley C. Canon argue in *Judicial Policies: Implementation and Impact* that the *Brown* decision "was a highly visible Court decision, a judicial attempt to generate one of the greatest social reforms in American history. And certainly in the years that followed, African Americans and their allies brought considerable pressures on other governmental bodies to desegregate the schools. Indeed, the pressures soon went far beyond schools to demand integration of all aspects of American life."

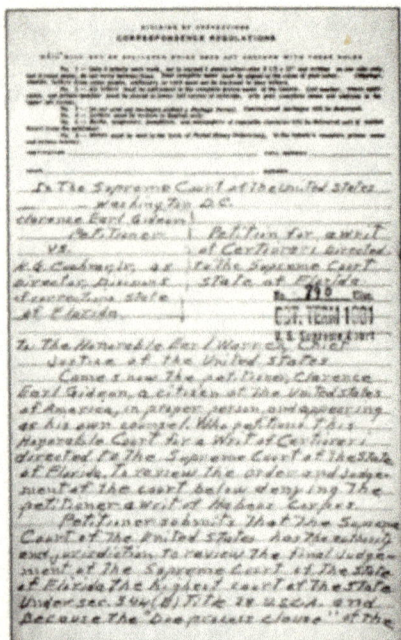

After Clarence Earl Gideon petitioned the Supreme Court that he had not had legal representation before a Florida court, the Justices ruled in 1963 that indigent defendants must be provided attorneys when they go to trial in felony cases.

Criminal Due Process

Judicial policy making in the area of criminal due process is most closely associated with Earl Warren's tenure as U.S. chief justice (1953-69). Speaking of this era, Archibald Cox, a former solicitor general, said, "Never has there been such a thorough-going reform of criminal procedure within so short a time." The Warren Court decisions were aimed primarily at changing the procedures followed by the states in dealing with criminal defendants. By the time Warren left the Supreme Court, new policies had been established to deal with a wide range of activities; among the more far-reaching were *Mapp v. Ohio* (1961), *Gideon v. Wainwright*, and *Miranda v. Arizona*.

The *Mapp* decision extended the exclusionary rule, which had applied to the national government for a number of years, to the states. This rule required state courts to exclude from trial evidence that had been illegally seized by the police. Although some police departments, especially in major urban areas, have tried to establish specific guidelines for their officers to follow in obtaining evidence, such efforts have not been universal. Because of variations in police practices and differing lower-court interpretations of what constitutes a valid search and seizure, implementation of *Mapp* has not been consistent throughout the United States.

U.S. Chief Justice Earl Warren, seen here in a 1961 photo. During his tenure, 1953-69, the Supreme Court sparked major reforms in criminal procedure through landmark decisions, including *Gideon v. Wainwright* and *Miranda v. Arizona*.

Perhaps even more important in reducing the expected impact of *Mapp* was the lack of solid support for the exclusionary rule among the Supreme Court justices. The decision was not a unanimous one to begin with, and over the years some justices have been openly critical of the exclusion-ary rule. Furthermore, subsequent Supreme Court decisions have broad-ened the scope of legal searches, thus limiting the applicability of the rule.

The *Gideon v. Wainwright* decision held that indigent defendants must be provided attorneys when they go to trial in a felony case in the state courts.

Many states routinely provided attorneys in such trials even before the Court's decision. The other states began to comply in a variety of ways. Public defender programs were established in many regions. In other areas, local bar associations cooperated with judges to implement some method of complying with the Supreme Court's new policy.

The impact of the *Gideon* decision is clearer and more consistent than that of *Mapp*. One reason, no doubt, is the fact that many states had already implemented the policy called for by *Gideon*. It was simply more widely accepted than the policy established by *Mapp*. The policy announced in *Gideon* was also more sharply defined than the one in *Mapp*. Although the Court did not specify whether a public defender or a court-appointed lawyer must be provided, it is still clear that the indigent defendant must have the help of an attorney. Also, the Supreme Court under the next chief justice, Warren Burger (1969-86), did not retreat from the Warren Court's policy of providing an attorney for indigent defendants as it did in the search and seizure area addressed by *Mapp*. All these factors add up to a more recognizable impact for the policy announced in *Gideon*.

In *Miranda v. Arizona* the Supreme Court went a step further and ruled that police officers must advise suspects taken into custody of their constitutional rights, one of which is to have an attorney present during questioning. Suspects must also be advised that they have a right to remain silent and that any statement they make may be used in court; that if they cannot afford an attorney, one will be provided at state expense; and that they have the right to stop answering questions at any time. These requirements are so clearly stated that police departments have actually copied them down on cards for officers to carry in their shirt pockets. Then, when suspects are taken into custody, the police officers simply remove the card and read the suspects their rights.

In terms of whether police officers read the *Miranda* rights to persons they arrest, there has been a high level of compliance with the Supreme Court policy. Some researchers, however, have questioned the impact of *Miranda* because of the method by which suspects may be advised of their rights. It is one thing to read to a person from a card; it is another to explain what is meant by the High Court's requirements and then try to make the suspect understand them. Looked at in this manner, the impact of the policy announced in *Miranda* is not quite as clear.

The Burger Court did not show an inclination to lend its solid support to the Warren Court's *Miranda* policy. Although *Miranda* has not been overruled, its impact has been limited somewhat. In *Harris v. New York* (1971), for example, the Burger Court ruled that statements made by an individual who had not been given the *Miranda* warning could be used to challenge the credibility of his testimony at trial. Then, the Court, under the leadership of Chief Justice William Rehnquist (1986-), ruled in *Davis v. United States* (1994) that police are not required to stop questioning a suspect who makes an ambiguous request to have an attorney present.

Congress reacted to *Miranda*, two years after the decision, by enacting a statute that in essence made the admissibility of a suspect's statements turn solely on whether they were made voluntarily. The statute received little attention until 1999 when the Fourth Circuit Court of Appeals, in a case involving an alleged bank robber who moved to suppress a statement he made to the FBI on grounds that he had not received "*Miranda* warnings" before being interrogated, held that the statute was satisfied because his statement was voluntary. The court of appeals decision raised the question whether the congressional statute or the High Court's *Miranda* decision should be followed. On June 26, 2000, the U.S. Supreme Court held that *Miranda*, being a constitutional decision of the Court, could not in effect be overruled by an act of Congress. In other words, the *Miranda* decision still governs the admissibility of statements made during custodial interrogation in state and federal courts.

In sum, the impact of the Supreme Court's criminal justice policies has been mixed, for several reasons. In some instances ambiguity is a problem. In other cases, less than solid support for the policy may be evident among justices or support erodes when one Court replaces another. All these variables translate into greater discretion for the implementers.

Abortion

In *Roe v. Wade* (1973) the Supreme Court ruled that a woman has an absolute right to an abortion during the first trimester of pregnancy; that a state may regulate the abortion procedure during the second trimester in order to protect the mother's health; and that, during the third trimester, the state may regulate or even prohibit abortions, except where the life or health of the mother is endangered.

The reaction to this decision was immediate, and primarily negative. It came in the form of letters to individual justices, public speeches, the introduction of resolutions in Congress, and the advocacy of "right to life" amendments in Congress. Given the controversial nature of the Court's decision, hospitals did not wholeheartedly offer to support the decision by changing their abortion policies.

Reaction to the Court's abortion policy has not only continued but also has moved into new areas. Recent presidential elections have seen the two major party platforms and candidates take opposing stands on the abortion issue. Democratic platforms and nominees have generally expressed support for *Roe v. Wade*, whereas the Republican platforms and contenders have noted opposition to the Supreme Court's decision.

Congress has also been a hotbed of activity in response to the Supreme Court's abortion decision. Unable to secure passage of a constitutional amendment to overturn *Roe v. Wade*, antiabortion — also known as pro-life — forces successfully lobbied for amendments to appropriations bills preventing the expenditure of federal funds for elective abortions. In 1980 the Supreme Court, in a five-to-four vote, upheld the constitutionality of such a prohibition.

Most of the legislation in the aftermath of the *Roe* decision has been at the state level. One study reports that within two years of the decision 32 states had passed 62 laws relating to abortion, most aimed at limiting access to abortions, regulating abortion procedures, or prohibiting abortions under certain conditions.

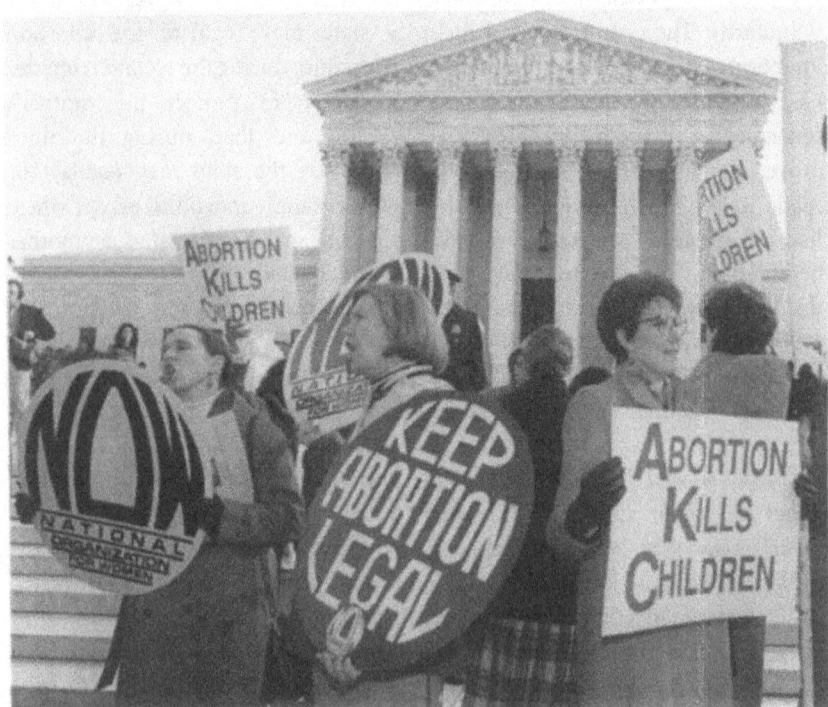

Since the Supreme Court's *Roe v. Wade* abortion ruling, the battles between supporters and opponents of abortion are being fought in Congress, at all levels of the judiciary, and in the political arena.

Interest group activity increased dramatically after the *Roe* decision. Groups opposing the decision often organized public demonstrations against the decision and later began to picket clinics. Interest groups that support the *Roe v. Wade* decision have been more likely to focus their efforts on the courts.

While battles over the abortion issue were being fought in the courts, political campaigns, and legislative arenas, others preferred a more direct approach, demonstrating at and blockading abortion centers. The Supreme Court has ruled, however, that reasonable time, place, and manner restrictions may be placed on such demonstrations. That position was reaffirmed on June 28, 2000, when the Court upheld a Colorado statute making it unlawful for a person to knowingly approach another person without that person's consent to hand out a leaflet, display a sign, or orally protest within 100 feet of a health care facility.

Conclusions

Some judicial policies have a greater impact on society than others. The judiciary plays a greater role in developing the nation's policies than the constitutional framers envisioned. However, "American courts are not all-powerful institutions," writes Gerald N. Rosenberg in *Hollow Hope: Can Courts Bring About Social Change?* "They were designed with severe limitations and placed in a political system of divided powers. To ask them to produce significant social reforms is to forget their history and ignore their constraints."

Within this complex framework of competing political and social demands and expectations is a policy-making role for the courts. Because the other two branches of government are sometimes not receptive to the demands of certain segments of society, the only alternative for those individuals or groups is to turn to the courts. Civil rights organizations, for example, made no real headway until they found the Supreme Court to be a supportive forum for their school desegregation efforts.

As civil rights groups attained some success in the federal courts, others were encouraged to employ litigation as a strategy. For example, women's rights supporters followed a pattern established by minority groups when they began taking their grievances to the courts. What began as a more narrow pursuit for racial equality was thus broadened to a quest for equality for other disadvantaged groups in society.

Clearly, then, the courts can announce policy decisions that attract national attention and perhaps stress the fact that other policy makers have failed to act. In this way the judiciary may invite the other branches to exercise their policy-making powers. Follow-up decisions indicate the judiciary's determination to pursue a particular policy and help keep alive the invitation for other policy makers to join in the endeavor.

All things considered, the courts seem best equipped to develop and implement narrow policies that are less controversial in nature. The policy established in the *Gideon* case provides a good example. The decision that indigent defendants in state criminal trials must be provided with an attorney did not meet any strong outcries of protest. Furthermore, it was a policy that primarily required the support of judges and lawyers; action by Congress and the president was not really necessary. A policy of equality for all segments of society, on the other hand, is so broad and controversy-laden that it must move beyond the judiciary. As it does so, the courts become simply one part, albeit an important part, of the policy-making process.   ⚖

THE CONSTITUTION OF THE UNITED STATES

The following text of the United States Constitution reflects the original spelling and usage. Brackets [ ] indicate parts that have been changed or set aside by amendments.

PREAMBLE:

We the People of the United States, in Order to form a more perfect Union, establish Justice, insure domestic Tranquility, provide for the common defence, promote the general Welfare, and secure the Blessings of Liberty to ourselves and our Posterity, do ordain and establish this Constitution for the United States of America.

ARTICLE. I.

Section. 1.

All legislative Powers herein granted shall be vested in a Congress of the United States, which shall consist of a Senate and House of Representatives.

Section. 2.

The House of Representatives shall be composed of Members chosen every second Year by the People of the several States, and the Electors in each State shall have the Qualifications requisite for Electors of the most numerous Branch of the State Legislature.

No Person shall be a Representative who shall not have attained to the Age of twenty five Years, and been seven Years a Citizen of the United States, and who shall not, when elected, be an Inhabitant of that State in which he shall be chosen.

Representatives and direct Taxes shall be apportioned among the several States [which may be included within this Union, according to their respective Numbers, which shall be determined by adding to the whole Number of free Persons, including those bound to Service for a Term of Years, and excluding Indians not taxed, three fifths of all other Persons.] The actual Enumeration shall be made within three Years after the first Meeting of the Congress of the United States, and within every subsequent Term of ten Years, in such Manner as they shall by Law direct. The number of Representatives shall not exceed one for every thirty Thousand, but each State shall have at Least one Representative; and until such enumeration shall be made, the State of New Hampshire shall be entitled to chuse three, Massachusetts eight, Rhode-Island and Providence Plantations one, Connecticut five, New-York six, New Jersey four, Pennsylvania eight, Delaware one, Maryland six, Virginia ten, North Carolina five, South Carolina five, and Georgia three.

When vacancies happen in the Representation from any State, the Executive Authority thereof shall issue Writs of Election to fill such Vacancies.

The House of Representatives shall chuse their Speaker and other Officers; and shall have the sole Power of Impeachment.

Section. 3.

The Senate of the United States shall be composed of two Senators from each State, [chosen by the Legislature thereof,] for six Years; and each Senator shall have one Vote.

Immediately after they shall be assembled in Consequence of the first Election, they shall be divided as equally as may be into three Classes. The Seats of the Senators of the first Class shall be vacated at the Expiration of the second Year, of the second Class at the Expiration of the fourth Year, and of the third Class at the Expiration of the sixth Year; so that one third may be chosen every second Year; [and if Vacancies happen by Resignation, or otherwise, during the Recess of the Legislature of any State, the Executive thereof may make temporary Appointments until the next Meeting of the Legislature, which shall then fill such Vacancies.]

No Person shall be a Senator who shall not have attained to the Age of thirty Years, and been nine Years a Citizen of the United States, and who shall not, when elected, be an Inhabitant of that State for which he shall be chosen.

The Vice President of the United States shall be President of the Senate, but shall have no Vote, unless they be equally divided.

The Senate shall chuse their other Officers, and also a President pro tempore, in the Absence of the Vice President, or when he shall exercise the Office of President of the United States.

The Senate shall have the sole Power to try all Impeachments. When sitting for that Purpose, they shall be on Oath or Affirmation. When the President of the United States is tried, the Chief Justice shall preside: And no Person shall be convicted without the Concurrence of two thirds of the Members present.

Judgment in Cases of Impeachment shall not extend further than to removal from Office, and disqualification to hold and enjoy any Office of honor, Trust or Profit under the United States: but the Party convicted shall nevertheless be liable and subject to Indictment, Trial, Judgment and Punishment, according to Law.

Section. 4.

The Times, Places and Manner of holding Elections for Senators and Representatives, shall be prescribed in each State by the Legislature thereof; but the Congress may at any time by Law make or alter such Regulations, [except as to the Places of chusing Senators.]

The Congress shall assemble at least once in every Year, [and such Meeting shall be on the first Monday in December,] unless they shall by Law appoint a different Day.

Section. 5.

Each House shall be the Judge of the Elections, Returns and Qualifications of its own Members, and a Majority of each shall constitute a Quorum to do Business; but a smaller Number may adjourn from day to day, and may be authorized to compel the Attendance of absent Members, in such Manner, and under such Penalties as each House may provide.

Each House may determine the Rules of its Proceedings, punish its Members for disorderly Behaviour; and, with the Concurrence of two thirds, expel a Member.

Each House shall keep a Journal of its Proceedings, and from time to time publish the same, excepting such Parts as may in their Judgment require Secrecy; and the Yeas and Nays of the Members of either House on any question shall, at the Desire of one fifth of those Present, be entered on the Journal.

Neither House, during the Session of Congress, shall, without the Consent of the other, adjourn for more than three days, nor to any other Place than that in which the two Houses shall be sitting.

Section. 6.

The Senators and Representatives shall receive a Compensation for their Services, to be ascertained by Law, and paid out of the Treasury of the United States. They shall in all Cases, except Treason, Felony and Breach of the Peace, be privileged from Arrest during their Attendance at the Session of their respective Houses, and in going to and returning from the same; and for any Speech or Debate in either House, they shall not be questioned in any other Place.

No Senator or Representative shall, during the Time for which he was elected, be appointed to any civil Office under the Authority of the United States, which shall have been created, or the Emoluments whereof shall have been encreased during such time; and no Person holding any Office under the United States, shall be a Member of either House during his Continuance in Office.

Section. 7.

All Bills for raising Revenue shall originate in the House of Representatives; but the Senate may propose or concur with Amendments as on other Bills.

Every Bill which shall have passed the House of Representatives and the Senate, shall, before it become a Law, be presented to the President of the United States; If he approve he shall sign it, but if not he shall return it, with his Objections to that House in which it shall have originated, who shall enter the Objections at large on their Journal, and proceed to reconsider it. If after such Reconsideration two thirds of that House shall agree to pass the Bill, it shall be sent, together with the Objections, to the other House, by which it shall likewise be reconsidered, and if approved by two thirds of that House, it shall become a Law. But in all such Cases the Votes of both Houses shall be determined by yeas and Nays, and the Names of the Persons voting for and against the Bill shall be entered on the Journal of each House respectively. If any Bill shall not be returned by the President within ten Days (Sundays excepted) after it shall have been presented to him, the Same shall be a Law, in like Manner as if he had signed it, unless the Congress by their Adjournment prevent its Return, in which Case it shall not be a Law.

Every Order, Resolution, or Vote to which the Concurrence of the Senate and House of Representatives may be necessary (except on a question of Adjournment) shall be presented to the President of the United States; and before the Same shall take Effect, shall be approved by him, or being disapproved by him, shall be repassed by two thirds of the Senate and House of Representatives, according to the Rules and Limitations prescribed in the Case of a Bill.

Section. 8.

The Congress shall have Power
To lay and collect Taxes, Duties, Imposts and Excises, to pay the Debts and provide for the common Defence and general Welfare of the United States; but all Duties, Imposts and Excises shall be uniform throughout the United States;

To borrow Money on the credit of the United States;

To regulate Commerce with foreign Nations, and among the several States, and with the Indian Tribes;

To establish an uniform Rule of Naturalization, and uniform Laws on the subject of Bankruptcies throughout the United States;

To coin Money, regulate the Value thereof, and of foreign Coin, and fix the Standard of Weights and Measures;

To provide for the Punishment of counterfeiting the Securities and current Coin of the United States;

To establish Post Offices and post Roads;

To promote the Progress of Science and useful Arts, by securing for limited Times to Authors and Inventors the exclusive Right to their respective Writings and Discoveries;

To constitute Tribunals inferior to the supreme Court;

To define and punish Piracies and Felonies committed on the high Seas, and Offences against the Law of Nations;

To declare War, grant Letters of Marque and Reprisal, and make Rules concerning Captures on Land and Water;

To raise and support Armies, but no Appropriation of Money to that Use shall be for a longer Term than two Years;

To provide and maintain a Navy;

To make Rules for the Government and Regulation of the land and naval Forces;

To provide for calling forth the Militia to execute the Laws of the Union, suppress Insurrections and repel Invasions;

To provide for organizing, arming, and disciplining, the Militia, and for governing such Part of them as may be employed in the Service of the United States, reserving to the States respectively, the Appointment of the Officers, and the Authority of training the Militia according to the discipline prescribed by Congress;

To exercise exclusive Legislation in all Cases whatsoever, over such District (not exceeding ten Miles square) as may, by Cession of particular States, and the Acceptance of Congress, become the Seat of the Government of the United States, and to exercise like Authority over all Places purchased by the Consent of the Legislature of the State in which the Same shall be, for the Erection of Forts, Magazines, Arsenals, dock-Yards, and other needful Buildings;—And

To make all Laws which shall be necessary and proper for carrying into Execution the foregoing Powers, and all other Powers vested by this Constitution in the Government of the United States, or in any Department or Officer thereof.

Section. 9.

The Migration or Importation of such Persons as any of the States now existing shall think proper to admit, shall not be prohibited by the Congress prior to the Year one thousand eight hundred and eight, but a Tax or duty may be imposed on such Importation, not exceeding ten dollars for each Person.

The Privilege of the Writ of Habeas Corpus shall not be suspended, unless when in Cases of Rebellion or Invasion the public Safety may require it.

No Bill of Attainder or ex post facto Law shall be passed.

No Capitation, [or other direct,] Tax shall be laid, unless in Proportion to the Census or Enumeration herein before directed to be taken.

No Tax or Duty shall be laid on Articles exported from any State.

No Preference shall be given by any Regulation of Commerce or Revenue to the Ports of one State over those of another: nor shall Vessels bound to, or from, one State, be obliged to enter, clear, or pay Duties in another.

No Money shall be drawn from the Treasury, but in Consequence of Appropriations made by Law; and a regular Statement and Account of the Receipts and Expenditures of all public Money shall be published from time to time.

No Title of Nobility shall be granted by the United States: And no Person holding any Office of Profit or Trust under them, shall, without the Consent of the Congress, accept of any present, Emolument, Office, or Title, of any kind whatever, from any King, Prince, or foreign State.

Section. 10.

No State shall enter into any Treaty, Alliance, or Confederation; grant Letters of Marque and Reprisal; coin Money; emit Bills of Credit; make any Thing but gold and silver Coin a Tender in Payment of Debts; pass any Bill of Attainder, ex post facto Law, or Law impairing the Obligation of Contracts, or grant any Title of Nobility.

No State shall, without the Consent of the Congress, lay any Imposts or Duties on Imports or Exports, except what may be absolutely necessary for executing it's inspection Laws: and the net Produce of all Duties and Imposts, laid by any State on Imports or Exports, shall be for the Use of the Treasury of the United States; and all such Laws shall be subject to the Revision and Controul of the Congress.

No State shall, without the Consent of Congress, lay any Duty of Tonnage, keep Troops, or Ships of War in time of Peace, enter into any Agreement or Compact with another State, or with a foreign Power, or engage in War, unless actually invaded, or in such imminent Danger as will not admit of delay.

ARTICLE. II.

Section. 1.

The executive Power shall be vested in a President of the United States of America. He shall hold his Office during the Term of four Years, and, together with the Vice President, chosen for the same Term, be elected, as follows

Each State shall appoint, in such Manner as the Legislature thereof may direct, a Number of Electors, equal to the whole Number of Senators and Representatives to which the State may be entitled in the Congress: but no Senator or Representative, or Person holding an Office of Trust or Profit under the United States, shall be appointed an Elector.

[The Electors shall meet in their respective States, and vote by Ballot for two Persons, of whom one at least shall not be an Inhabitant of the same State with themselves. And they shall make a List of all the Persons voted for, and of the Number of Votes for each; which List they shall sign and certify, and transmit sealed to the Seat of the Government of the United States, directed to the President of the Senate. The President of the Senate shall, in the Presence of the Senate and House of Representatives, open all the Certificates, and the Votes shall then be counted. The Person having the greatest Number of Votes shall be the President, if such Number be a Majority of the whole Number of Electors appointed; and if there be more than one who have such Majority, and have an equal Number of Votes, then the House of Representatives shall immediately chuse by Ballot one of them for President; and if no Person have a Majority, then from the five highest on the List the said House shall in like Manner chuse the President. But in chusing the President, the Votes shall be taken by States, the Representation from each State having one Vote; A quorum for this Purpose shall consist of a Member or Members from two thirds of the States, and a Majority of all the States shall be necessary to a Choice. In every Case, after the Choice of the President, the Person having the greatest Number of Votes of the Electors shall be the Vice President. But if there should remain two or more who have equal Votes, the Senate shall chuse from them by Ballot the Vice President.]

The Congress may determine the Time of chusing the Electors, and the Day on which they shall give their Votes; which Day shall be the same throughout the United States.

No Person except a natural born Citizen, or a Citizen of the United States, at the time of the Adoption of this Constitution, shall be eligible to the Office of President; neither shall any person be eligible to that Office who shall not have attained to the Age of thirty five Years, and been fourteen Years a Resident within the United States.

In Case of the Removal of the President from Office, or of his Death, Resignation, or Inability to discharge the Powers and Duties of the said Office, the Same shall devolve on the Vice President, and the Congress may by Law provide for the Case of Removal, Death, Resignation or Inability, both of the President and Vice President, declaring what Officer shall then act as President, and such Officer shall act accordingly, until the Disability be removed, or a President shall be elected.

The President shall, at stated Times, receive for his Services, a Compensation, which shall neither be increased nor diminished during the Period for which he shall have been elected, and he shall not receive within that Period any other Emolument from the United States, or any of them.

Before he enter on the Execution of his Office, he shall take the following Oath or Affirmation: — "I do solemnly swear (or affirm) that I will faithfully execute the Office of President of the United States, and will to the best of my Ability, preserve, protect and defend the Constitution of the United States."

Section. 2.

The President shall be Commander in Chief of the Army and Navy of the United States, and of the Militia of the several States, when called into the actual Service of the United States; he may require the Opinion, in writing, of the principal Officer in each of the executive Departments, upon any Subject relating to the Duties of their respective Offices, and he shall have Power to grant Reprieves and Pardons for Offences against the United States, except in Cases of Impeachment.

He shall have Power, by and with the Advice and Consent of the Senate, to make Treaties, provided two thirds of the Senators present concur; and he shall nominate, and by and with the Advice and Consent of the Senate, shall appoint Ambassadors, other public Ministers and Consuls, Judges of the supreme Court, and all other Officers of the United States, whose Appointments are not herein otherwise provided for, and which shall be established by Law: but the Congress may by Law vest the Appointment of such inferior Officers, as they think proper, in the President alone, in the Courts of Law, or in the Heads of Departments.

The President shall have Power to fill up all Vacancies that may happen during the Recess of the Senate, by granting Commissions which shall expire at the End of their next Session.

Section. 3.

He shall from time to time give to the Congress Information of the State of the Union, and recommend to their Consideration such Measures as he shall judge necessary and expedient; he may, on extraordinary Occasions, convene both Houses, or either of them, and in Case of Disagreement between them, with Respect to the Time of Adjournment, he may adjourn them to such

Time as he shall think proper; he shall receive Ambassadors and other public Ministers; he shall take Care that the Laws be faithfully executed, and shall Commission all the Officers of the United States.

Section. 4.

The President, Vice President and all civil Officers of the United States, shall be removed from Office on Impeachment for, and Conviction of, Treason, Bribery, or other high Crimes and Misdemeanors.

ARTICLE. III.

Section. 1.

The judicial Power of the United States, shall be vested in one supreme Court, and in such inferior Courts as the Congress may from time to time ordain and establish. The Judges, both of the supreme and inferior Courts, shall hold their Offices during good Behaviour; and shall, at stated Times, receive for their Services, a Compensation, which shall not be diminished during their Continuance in Office.

Section. 2.

The judicial Power shall extend to all Cases, in Law and Equity, arising under this Constitution, the Laws of the United States, and Treaties made, or which shall be made, under their Authority;— to all Cases affecting Ambassadors, other public Ministers and Consuls;— to all Cases of admiralty and maritime Jurisdiction;— to Controversies to which the United States shall be a Party;— to Controversies between two or more States;— [between a State and Citizens of another State;]— between Citizens of different States,— between Citizens of the same State claiming Lands under Grants of different States, and between a State, or the Citizens thereof, and foreign States, [Citizens or Subjects.]

In all Cases affecting Ambassadors, other public Ministers and Consuls, and those in which a State shall be Party, the supreme Court shall have original Jurisdiction. In all the other Cases before mentioned, the supreme Court shall have appellate Jurisdiction, both as to Law and Fact, with such Exceptions, and under such Regulations as the Congress shall make.

The Trial of all Crimes, except in Cases of Impeachment, shall be by Jury; and such Trial shall be held in the State where the said Crimes shall have been committed; but when not committed within any State, the Trial shall be at such Place or Places as the Congress may by Law have directed.

Section. 3.

Treason against the United States, shall consist only in levying War against them, or in adhering to their Enemies, giving them Aid and Comfort. No Person shall be convicted of Treason unless on the Testimony of two Witnesses to the same overt Act, or on Confession in open Court.

The Congress shall have Power to declare the Punishment of Treason, but no Attainder of Treason shall work Corruption of Blood, or Forfeiture except during the Life of the Person attainted.

ARTICLE. IV.

Section. 1.

Full Faith and Credit shall be given in each State to the public Acts, Records, and judicial Proceedings of every other State. And the Congress may by general Laws prescribe the Manner in which such Acts, Records and Proceedings shall be proved, and the Effect thereof.

Section. 2.

The Citizens of each State shall be entitled to all Privileges and Immunities of Citizens in the several States.

A Person charged in any State with Treason, Felony, or other Crime, who shall flee from Justice, and be found in another State, shall on Demand of the executive Authority of the State from which he fled, be delivered up, to be removed to the State having Jurisdiction of the Crime.

[No Person held to Service or Labour in one State, under the Laws thereof, escaping into another, shall, in Consequence of any Law or Regulation therein, be discharged from such Service or Labour, but shall be delivered up on Claim of the Party to whom such Service or Labour may be due.]

Section. 3.

New States may be admitted by the Congress into this Union; but no new State shall be formed or erected within the Jurisdiction of any other State; nor any State be formed by the Junction of two or more States, or Parts of States, without the Consent of the Legislatures of the States concerned as well as of the Congress.

The Congress shall have Power to dispose of and make all needful Rules and Regulations respecting the Territory or other Property belonging to the United States; and nothing in this Constitution shall be so construed as to Prejudice any Claims of the United States, or of any particular State.

Section. 4.

The United States shall guarantee to every State in this Union a Republican Form of Government, and shall protect each of them against Invasion; and on Application of the Legislature, or of the Executive (when the Legislature cannot be convened) against domestic Violence.

ARTICLE. V.

The Congress, whenever two thirds of both Houses shall deem it necessary, shall propose Amendments to this Constitution, or, on the Application of the Legislatures of two thirds of the several States, shall call a Convention for proposing Amendments, which, in either Case, shall be valid to all Intents and Purposes, as Part of this Constitution, when ratified by the Legislatures of three fourths of the several States, or by Conventions in three fourths thereof, as the one or the other Mode of Ratification may be proposed by the Congress; Provided [that no Amendment which may be made prior to the Year One thousand eight hundred and eight shall in any Manner affect the first and fourth Clauses in the Ninth Section of the first Article; and] that no State, without its Consent, shall be deprived of its equal Suffrage in the Senate.

ARTICLE. VI.

All Debts contracted and Engagements entered into, before the Adoption of this Constitution, shall be as valid against the United States under this Constitution, as under the Confederation.

This Constitution, and the Laws of the United States which shall be made in Pursuance thereof; and all Treaties made, or which shall be made, under the Authority of the United States, shall be the supreme Law of the Land; and the Judges in every State shall be bound thereby, any Thing in the Constitution or Laws of any State to the Contrary notwithstanding.

The Senators and Representatives before mentioned, and the Members of the several State Legislatures, and all executive and judicial Officers, both of the United States and of the several States, shall be bound by Oath or Affirmation, to support this Constitution; but no religious Test shall ever be required as a Qualification to any Office or public Trust under the United States.

ARTICLE. VII.

The Ratification of the Conventions of nine States, shall be sufficient for the Establishment of this Constitution between the States so ratifying the Same.

(The following statement reflects copyist's corrections to the original document.)

The Word, "the," being interlined between the seventh and eighth Lines of the first Page, The Word "Thirty" being partly written on an Erazure in the fifteenth Line of the first Page, The Words "is tried" being interlined between the thirty second and thirty third Lines of the first Page and the Word "the" being interlined between the forty third and forty fourth Lines of the second Page.

Attest William Jackson Secretary

done in Convention by the Unanimous Consent of the States present the Seventeenth Day of September in the Year of our Lord one thousand seven hundred and Eighty seven and of the Independence of the United States of America the Twelfth
In witness whereof We have hereunto subscribed our Names,

Go. WASHINGTON — Presid.t
and deputy from Virginia

Delaware
Geo: Read
Gunning Bedford jun
John Dickinson
Richard Bassett
Jaco: Broom

Maryland
James McHenry
Dan of St Thos: Jenifer
Danl Carroll

Virginia
John Blair—
James Madison Jr.

North Carolina
Wm. Blount
Richd. Dobbs Spaight
Hu Williamson

South Carolina
J. Rutledge
Charles Cotesworth Pinckney
Charles Pinckney
Pierce Butler

Georgia
William Few
Abr Baldwin

New Hampshire
John Langdon
Nicholas Gilman

Massachusetts
Nathaniel Gorham
Rufus King

Connecticut
Wm. Saml. Johnson
Roger Sherman

New York
Alexander Hamilton

New Jersey
Wil: Livingston
David Brearley.
Wm. Paterson.
Jona: Dayton

Pennsylvania
B Franklin
Thomas Mifflin
Robt Morris
Geo. Clymer
Thos. FitzSimons
Jared Ingersoll
James Wilson
Gouv Morris

AMENDMENTS TO THE CONSTITUTION OF THE UNITED STATES

(The first ten amendments, known as the Bill of Rights, were ratified in 1791.)

The Preamble to The Bill of Rights

Congress of the United States
begun and held at the City of New-York, on
Wednesday the fourth of March, one thousand seven hundred and eighty nine.

THE Conventions of a number of the States, having at the time of their adopting the Constitution, expressed a desire, in order to prevent misconstruction or abuse of its powers, that further declaratory and restrictive clauses should be added: And as extending the ground of public confidence in the Government, will best ensure the beneficent ends of its institution.

RESOLVED by the Senate and House of Representatives of the United States of America, in Congress assembled, two thirds of both Houses concurring, that the following Articles be proposed to the Legislatures of the several States, as amendments to the Constitution of the United States, all, or any of which Articles, when ratified by three fourths of the said Legislatures, to be valid to all intents and purposes, as part of the said Constitution; viz.

ARTICLES in addition to, and Amendment of the Constitution of the United States of America, proposed by Congress, and ratified by the Legislatures of the several States, pursuant to the fifth Article of the original Constitution.

AMENDMENT I

Congress shall make no law respecting an establishment of religion, or prohibiting the free exercise thereof; or abridging the freedom of speech, or of the press; or the right of the people peaceably to assemble, and to petition the Government for a redress of grievances.

AMENDMENT II

A well regulated Militia, being necessary to the security of a free State, the right of the people to keep and bear Arms, shall not be infringed.

AMENDMENT III

No Soldier shall, in time of peace be quartered in any house, without the consent of the Owner; nor in time of war, but in a manner to be prescribed by law.

AMENDMENT IV

The right of the people to be secure in their persons, houses, papers, and effects, against unreasonable searches and seizures, shall not be violated, and no Warrants shall issue, but upon probable cause, supported by Oath or affirmation, and particularly describing the place to be searched, and the persons or things to be seized.

AMENDMENT V

No person shall be held to answer for a capital, or otherwise infamous crime, unless on a presentment or indictment of a Grand Jury, except in cases arising in the land or naval forces, or in the Militia, when in actual service in time of War or public danger; nor shall any person be subject for the same offence to be twice put in jeopardy of life or limb; nor shall be compelled in any criminal case to be a witness against himself, nor be deprived of life, liberty, or property, without due process of law; nor shall private property be taken for public use without just compensation.

AMENDMENT VI

In all criminal prosecutions, the accused shall enjoy the right to a speedy and public trial, by an impartial jury of the State and district wherein the crime shall have been committed, which district shall have been previously ascertained by law, and to be informed of the nature and cause of the accusation; to be confronted with the witnesses against him; to have compulsory process for obtaining witnesses in his favor, and to have the Assistance of Counsel for his defence.

AMENDMENT VII

In Suits at common law, where the value in controversy shall exceed twenty dollars, the right of trial by jury shall be preserved, and no fact tried by a jury, shall be otherwise re-examined in any Court of the United States, than according to the rules of the common law.

AMENDMENT VIII

Excessive bail shall not be required, nor excessive fines imposed, nor cruel and unusual punishments inflicted.

AMENDMENT IX

The enumeration in the Constitution, of certain rights, shall not be construed to deny or disparage others retained by the people.

AMENDMENT X

The powers not delegated to the United States by the Constitution, nor prohibited by it to the States, are reserved to the States respectively, or to the people.

AMENDMENT XI (1795)

The Judicial power of the United States shall not be construed to extend to any suit in law or equity, commenced or prosecuted against one of the United States by Citizens of another State, or by Citizens or Subjects of any Foreign State.

AMENDMENT XII (1804)

The Electors shall meet in their respective states, and vote by ballot for President and Vice-President, one of whom, at least, shall not be an inhabitant of the same state with themselves; they shall name in their ballots the person voted for as President, and in distinct ballots the person voted for as Vice-President, and they shall make distinct lists of all persons voted for as President, and of all persons voted for as Vice-President, and of the number of votes for each, which lists they shall sign and certify, and transmit sealed to the seat of the government of the United States, directed to the President of the Senate;—The President of the Senate shall, in the presence of the Senate and House of Representatives, open all the certificates and the votes shall then be counted;—The person having the greatest number of votes for President, shall be the President, if such number be a majority of the whole number of Electors appointed; and if no person have such majority, then from the persons having the highest numbers not exceeding three on the list of those voted for as President, the House of Representatives shall choose immediately, by ballot, the President. But in choosing the President, the votes shall be taken by states, the representation from each state having one vote; a quorum for this purpose shall consist of a member or members from two-thirds of the states, and a majority of all the states shall be necessary to a choice. {And if the House of Representatives shall not choose a President whenever the right of choice shall devolve upon them, before the fourth day of March next following, then the Vice-President shall act as President, as in the case of the death or other constitutional disability of the President}* — The person having the greatest number of votes as Vice-President, shall be the Vice-President, if such number be a majority of the whole number of Electors appointed, and if no person have a majority, then from the two highest numbers on the list, the Senate shall choose the Vice-President; a quorum for the purpose shall consist of two-thirds of the whole number of Senators, and a majority of the whole number shall be necessary to a choice. But no person constitutionally ineligible to the office of President shall be eligible to that of Vice-President of the United States.

*Superseded by Section 3 of the Twentieth Amendment.

AMENDMENT XIII (1865)

Section 1.
Neither slavery nor involuntary servitude, except as a punishment for crime whereof the party shall have been duly convicted, shall exist within the United States, or any place subject to their jurisdiction.

Section 2.
Congress shall have power to enforce this article by appropriate legislation.

AMENDMENT XIV (1868)

Section 1.

All persons born or naturalized in the United States and subject to the jurisdiction thereof, are citizens of the United States and of the State wherein they reside. No State shall make or enforce any law which shall abridge the privileges or immunities of citizens of the United States; nor shall any State deprive any person of life, liberty, or property, without due process of law; nör deny to any person within its jurisdiction the equal protection of the laws.

Section 2.

Representatives shall be apportioned among the several States according to their respective numbers, counting the whole number of persons in each State, [excluding Indians not taxed.] But when the right to vote at any election for the choice of electors for President and Vice President of the United States, Representatives in Congress, the Executive and Judicial officers of a State, or the members of the Legislature thereof, is denied to any of the male inhabitants of such State, being twenty-one years of age,* and citizens of the United States, or in any way abridged, except for participation in rebellion, or other crime, the basis of representation therein shall be reduced in the proportion which the number of such male citizens shall bear to the whole number of male citizens twenty-one years of age in such State.

*Changed by Section 1 of the Twenty-sixth Amendment.

Section 3.

No person shall be a Senator or Representative in Congress, or elector of President and Vice President, or hold any office, civil or military, under the United States, or under any State, who, having previously taken an oath, as a member of Congress, or as an officer of the United States, or as a member of any State legislature, or as an executive or judicial officer of any State, to support the Constitution of the United States, shall have engaged in insurrection or rebellion against the same, or given aid or comfort to the enemies thereof. But Congress may by a vote of two-thirds of each House, remove such disability.

Section 4.

The validity of the public debt of the United States, authorized by law, including debts incurred for payment of pensions and bounties for services in suppressing insurrection or rebellion, shall not be questioned. But neither the United States nor any State shall assume or pay any debt or obligation incurred in aid of insurrection or rebellion against the United States, or any claim for the loss or emancipation of any slave; but all such debts, obligations and claims shall be held illegal and void.

Section 5.

The Congress shall have power to enforce, by appropriate legislation, the provisions of this article.

AMENDMENT XV (1870)

Section 1.

The right of citizens of the United States to vote shall not be denied or abridged by the United States or by any State on account of race, color, or previous condition of servitude.

Section 2.

The Congress shall have power to enforce this article by appropriate legislation.

AMENDMENT XVI (1913)

The Congress shall have power to lay and collect taxes on incomes, from whatever source derived, without apportionment among the several States, and without regard to any census or enumeration.

AMENDMENT XVII (1913)

The Senate of the United States shall be composed of two Senators from each State, elected by the people thereof, for six years; and each Senator shall have one vote. The electors in each State shall have the qualifications requisite for electors of the most numerous branch of the State legislatures.

When vacancies happen in the representation of any State in the Senate, the executive authority of such State shall issue writs of election to fill such vacancies: Provided, That the legislature of any State may empower the executive thereof to make temporary appointments until the people fill the vacancies by election as the legislature may direct.

This amendment shall not be so construed as to affect the election or term of any Senator chosen before it becomes valid as part of the Constitution.

AMENDMENT XVIII (1919, repealed by Amendment XXI)

Section 1.

After one year from the ratification of this article the manufacture, sale, or transportation of intoxicating liquors within, the importation thereof into, or the exportation thereof from the United States and all territory subject to the jurisdiction thereof for beverage purposes is hereby prohibited.

Section 2.

The Congress and the several States shall have concurrent power to enforce this article by appropriate legislation.

Section 3.

This article shall be inoperative unless it shall have been ratified as an amendment to the Constitution by the legislatures of the several States, as provided in the Constitution, within seven years from the date of the submission hereof to the States by the Congress.

AMENDMENT XIX (1920)

The right of citizens of the United States to vote shall not be denied or abridged by the United States or by any State on account of sex.

Congress shall have power to enforce this article by appropriate legislation.

AMENDMENT XX (1933)

Section 1.

The terms of the President and Vice President shall end at noon on the 20th day of January, and the terms of Senators and Representatives at noon on the 3d day of January, of the years in which such terms would have ended if this article had not been ratified; and the terms of their successors shall then begin.

Section 2.

The Congress shall assemble at least once in every year, and such meeting shall begin at noon on the 3d day of January, unless they shall by law appoint a different day.

Section 3.

If, at the time fixed for the beginning of the term of the President, the President elect shall have died, the Vice President elect shall become President. If a President shall not have been chosen before the time fixed for the beginning of his term, or if the President elect shall have failed to qualify, then the Vice President elect shall act as President until a President shall have qualified; and the Congress may by law provide for the case wherein neither a President elect nor a Vice President elect shall have qualified, declaring who shall then act as President, or the manner in which one who is to act shall be selected, and such person shall act accordingly until a President or Vice President shall have qualified.

Section 4.

The Congress may by law provide for the case of the death of any of the persons from whom the House of Representatives may choose a President whenever the right of choice shall have devolved upon them, and for the case of the death of any of the persons from whom the Senate may choose a Vice President whenever the right of choice shall have devolved upon them.

Section 5.

Sections 1 and 2 shall take effect on the 15th day of October following the ratification of this article.

Section 6.

This article shall be inoperative unless it shall have been ratified as an amendment to the Constitution by the legislatures of three-fourths of the several States within seven years from the date of its submission.

AMENDMENT XXI (1933)

Section 1.

The eighteenth article of amendment to the Constitution of the United States is hereby repealed.

Section 2.
The transportation or importation into any State, Territory, or possession of the United States for delivery or use therein of intoxicating liquors, in violation of the laws thereof, is hereby prohibited.

Section 3.

This article shall be inoperative unless it shall have been ratified as an amendment to the Constitution by conventions in the several States, as provided in the Constitution, within seven years from the date of the submission hereof to the States by the Congress.

AMENDMENT XXII (1951)

Section 1.

No person shall be elected to the office of the President more than twice, and no person who has held the office of President, or acted as President, for more than two years of a term to which some other person was elected President shall be elected to the office of the President more than once. But this article shall not apply to any person holding the office of President when this article was proposed by the Congress, and shall not prevent any person who may be holding the office of President, or acting as President, during the term within which this article becomes operative from holding the office of President or acting as President during the remainder of such term.

Section 2.

This article shall be inoperative unless it shall have been ratified as an amendment to the Constitution by the legislatures of three-fourths of the several states within seven years from the date of its submission to the states by the Congress.

AMENDMENT XXIII (1961)

Section 1.

The District constituting the seat of government of the United States shall appoint in such manner as the Congress may direct:

A number of electors of President and Vice President equal to the whole number of Senators and Representatives in Congress to which the District would be entitled if it were a state, but in no event more than the least populous state; they shall be in addition to those appointed by the states, but they shall be considered, for the purposes of the election of President and Vice President, to be electors appointed by a state; and they shall meet in the District and perform such duties as provided by the twelfth article of amendment.

Section 2.

The Congress shall have power to enforce this article by appropriate legislation.

AMENDMENT XXIV (1964)

Section 1.

The right of citizens of the United States to vote in any primary or other election for President or Vice President, for electors for President or Vice

President, or for Senator or Representative in Congress, shall not be denied or abridged by the United States or any state by reason of failure to pay any poll tax or other tax.

Section 2.

The Congress shall have power to enforce this article by appropriate legislation.

AMENDMENT XXV (1967)

Section 1.

In case of the removal of the President from office or of his death or resignation, the Vice President shall become President.

Section 2.

Whenever there is a vacancy in the office of the Vice President, the President shall nominate a Vice President who shall take office upon confirmation by a majority vote of both Houses of Congress.

Section 3.

Whenever the President transmits to the President pro tempore of the Senate and the Speaker of the House of Representatives his written declaration that he is unable to discharge the powers and duties of his office, and until he transmits to them a written declaration to the contrary, such powers and duties shall be discharged by the Vice President as Acting President.

Section 4.

Whenever the Vice President and a majority of either the principal officers of the executive departments or of such other body as Congress may by law provide, transmit to the President pro tempore of the Senate and the Speaker of the House of Representatives their written declaration that the President is unable to discharge the powers and duties of his office, the Vice President shall immediately assume the powers and duties of the office as Acting President.

Thereafter, when the President transmits to the President pro tempore of the Senate and the Speaker of the House of Representatives his written declaration that no inability exists, he shall resume the powers and duties of his office unless the Vice President and a majority of either the principal officers of the executive department or of such other body as Congress may by law provide, transmit within four days to the President pro tempore of the Senate and the Speaker of the House of Representatives their written declaration that the President is unable to discharge the powers and duties of his office. Thereupon Congress shall decide the issue, assembling within forty-eight hours for that purpose if not in session. If the Congress, within twenty-one days after receipt of the latter written declaration, or, if Congress is not in session, within twenty-one days after Congress is required to assemble, determines by two-thirds vote of both Houses that the President is unable to discharge the powers and duties of his office, the Vice President shall continue to discharge the same as Acting President; otherwise, the President shall resume the powers and duties of his office.

AMENDMENT XXVI (1971)

Section 1.

The right of citizens of the United States, who are 18 years of age or older, to vote, shall not be denied or abridged by the United States or any State on account of age.

Section 2.

The Congress shall have the power to enforce this article by appropriate legislation.

AMENDMENT XXVII (1992)

No law, varying the compensation for the services of the Senators and Representatives, shall take effect, until an election of Representatives shall have intervened.

GLOSSARY

Activism (judicial). The willingness of a judge to inject into a case his or her own personal values about what is good and bad public policy. See also self-restraint (judicial).

Actus reus. The material element of the crime, which may be the commission of a forbidden action (for example, robbery) or the failure to perform a required action (for example, to stop and render aid to a motor vehicle accident victim).

Adversarial process. The process used in American courtrooms where the trial is seen as a battle between two opposing sides, and the role of the judge is to act as a sort of passive referee. See also inquisitorial method.

Advisory opinions. Rendering a decision on an abstract or hypothetical question (something that American courts are not supposed to do).

Alternative dispute resolution (ADR). Methods of resolving disputes (often with the help of neutral third parties) without a trial. Mediation and arbitration are two well-known ADR techniques.

Amicus curiae. ("Friend of the court.") A person (or group), not a party to a case, who submits views (usually in the form of written briefs) about how the case should be decided.

Answer. The formal written statement by a defendant responding to a civil complaint and setting forth the grounds for his or her defense.

Appellate jurisdiction. The authority of a higher court to review the decision of a lower court.

Arraignment. The process in which the defendant is brought before the judge in the court where he or she is to be tried to respond to the grand jury indictment or the prosecutor's bill of information.

Bail. A sum of money put up with the court by the defendant to ensure that he or she will appear at the time of trial.

Bench trial. Trial without a jury in which the judge decides which party prevails.

Bill of attainder. A law, forbidden by the U.S. Constitution, that makes conduct illegal for one person (or class of persons) but not for the population in general.

Bill of information. A statement of the charges against the accused prepared by the prosecutor, which, if approved by a judge, will require the accused to stand trial for the alleged crimes. This is used in states that do not employ a grand jury.

Certification. The procedure by which one of the U.S. appeals courts asks the U.S. Supreme Court for instructions or clarification about a particular legal matter. Either the justices may choose to honor this request or not, or they may request that the entire record of the case be sent to the Supreme Court for review and final judgment.

Civil law. The law that pertains to the relationship between one private citizen and another, between a private citizen and a corporation, or between one corporation and another.

Class action. A suit brought by persons having similar grievances against a common entity; for example, a group of smokers with lung cancer suing a tobacco company.

Collegial courts. Courts having more than one judge, which are almost always appellate courts.

Common law. A system of law inherited from England based on legal precedents or tradition instead of statutory law or systematic legal codes.

Complaint. A written statement filed by the plaintiff that initiates a civil case. It states the wrongs allegedly committed by the defendant and requests relief from the court.

Concurrent jurisdiction. A situation in which two courts have a legal right to hear the same case. For example, both the U.S. Supreme Court and U.S. trial courts have concurrent jurisdiction in certain cases brought by or against ambassadors or counsels.

Concurring opinion. An opinion by a member of a court that agrees with the result reached in a case but offers its own rationale for the decision.

Corpus juris. The entire body of law for a particular legal entity.

Courtroom workgroup. The regular participants in the day-to-day activities of a particular courtroom. The most visible members of this group are judges, prosecutors, and defense attorneys.

Court of appeals. A court that is higher than an ordinary trial court and has the function of reviewing or correcting the decisions of trial judges.

Crime. An offense against the state punishable by fine, imprisonment, or death.

Criminal law. The law that pertains to offenses against the state itself, actions that may be directed against a person but that are deemed to be offensive to society as a whole — for example, armed robbery or rape.

Cross-examination. During a trial, the questions posed to a witness who has been called to the stand by the opposing attorney.

Damages. Money paid by defendants to successful plaintiffs in civil cases to compensate the plaintiffs for their injuries. Compensatory damages are designed to cover the plaintiff's actual loss; punitive damages are designed to punish the defendant.

Declaratory judgment. When a court outlines the rights of the parties under a statute, a will, or a contract.

Defendant. In a civil case, the person or organization against whom the plaintiff brings suit; in a criminal case, the person accused of the crime.

Deposition. An oral statement made before an officer authorized by law to administer oaths. Such statements are often taken to examine potential witnesses in the discovery process.

Discovery. The process by which lawyers learn about their opponent's case in preparation for trial. Typical tools of discovery include depositions, interrogatories, and requests for documents.

Dissenting opinion. An opinion by a member of a court that disagrees with the result reached in the case by the court.

Diversity of citizenship suit. A civil legal proceeding brought by a citizen of one state against a citizen of another state.

En banc. ("In the bench" or "as a full bench.") Court sessions with the entire membership of a court participating, not just a smaller panel of judges.

Equity. That realm of the law in which the judge is able to issue a remedy that will either prevent or cure the wrong that is about to happen; for example, an injunction against an illegal strike by a union.

Ex post facto law. Forbidden by the U.S. Constitution, this law declares conduct to be illegal after the conduct takes place.

Federal question. If a court case centers around the interpretation of a federal law, the U.S. Constitution, or a treaty, then it contains a federal question and the case may be heard by a U.S. court.

Felony. Any offense for which the penalty may be death or imprisonment in a penitentiary.

Grand jury. A body of 16 to 23 citizens who listen to evidence of criminal allegations, which is presented by the prosecutors, and determine whether probable cause exists to believe an individual committed an offense. See also indictment.

Habeas corpus. A writ (court order) that is usually used to bring a prisoner before the court to determine the legality of his or her imprisonment.

Impeachment. The only way in which a federal judge may be removed from office. The House of Representatives brings the charge(s), and the Senate, following trial, convicts by a two-thirds vote of the membership.

Indictment. The decision of a grand jury to order a defendant to stand trial because the jury believes that probable cause exists to warrant a trial.

Inquisitorial method. The procedure used in most European and Latin American courtrooms in which the judge and jury take an active role in the trial and the attorneys act only to aid and supplement the judicial inquiry. See also adversarial process.

Interrogatories. Written questions sent by one party in a lawsuit to an opposing party as part of pretrial discovery in civil cases. The party receiving the interrogatories is required to answer them in writing under oath.

Judgment. The official decision of a court finally resolving the dispute between the parties to the lawsuit.

Judicial review. The power of the judicial branch to declare acts of the executive and legislative branches unconstitutional.

Jurisdiction. The authority of a court to hear and decide legal disputes and to enforce its rulings.

Justiciability. Whether a judge ought to hear or refrain from hearing certain types of cases. It differs from jurisdiction, which pertains to the technical right of a judge to hear a case. For example, lawsuits dealing with political questions are considered nonjusticiable.

Law. A social norm that is sanctioned in threat or in fact by the application of physical force. The party that exercises such physical force is recognized by society as legitimately having this kind of authority, such as a police officer.

Magistrate. A lower level judicial official to whom the accused is brought after the arrest. A magistrate has the obligation of informing the accused of the charges against him or her and of his or her legal rights.

Mandatory sentencing laws. Statutes that require automatic jail time for a convicted criminal, usually for a minimum period of time. These laws are often for violent crimes in which a gun was used and for habitual offenders.

Mens rea. The mental element of the crime — that is, what was intended by the perpetrator of the crime. Usually the more intentional and willful the mental state, the more serious the crime.

Merit selection. A method of selecting state judges that requires the governor to make the appointment from a short list of names submitted by a special commission established for that purpose. After serving for a short period of time, the judge must run in a retention election. Voters thus determine whether the judge should be retained for a full term.

Misdemeanor. A petty crime. Punishment usually is confinement in a city or county jail for less than a year.

Moot. Describes a case when the basic facts or the status of the parties have significantly changed in the interim when the suit was filed and when it comes before the judge.

Nolo contendere. ("No contest.") A plea by a criminal defendant in which he or she does not deny the facts of the case but claims that he or she has not committed any crime, or it may mean that the defendant does not understand the charges.

Opinion of the court. A judge's written explanation of the court's decision. Because the case may be heard by a panel of judges in an appellate court, the opinion can take two forms. If all the judges completely agree with the result, one judge will write the opinion for all. If all the judges do not agree, the formal decision will be based on the view of the majority, and one member of the majority will write the decision.

Oral argument. An opportunity for lawyers to summarize their position before the court and to answer the judges' questions.

Ordinance-making power. The power of state governors to fill in the details of legislation passed by state legislatures.

Original jurisdiction. The court that by law must be the first to hear a particular type of case. For example, in suits with at least $75,000 at stake between citizens from different states, the federal district courts are the courts of original jurisdiction.

Overcharging. The process whereby a prosecutor charges a criminal defendant with crimes more serious than the facts warrant to obtain a more favorable plea bargain from the defendant's attorney.

Per curiam. ("By the court.") An unsigned opinion of the court, often brief.

Peremptory challenge. An objection that an attorney might have to a prospective juror. The juror may be eliminated from the array without the attorney having to give a public reason for the objection. The number of such challenges is limited by law.

Petit jury (or trial jury). A group of citizens who hear the evidence presented by both sides at trial and determine the facts in dispute.

Plaintiff. The person who files the complaint in a civil lawsuit.

Plea bargain. A bargain or deal that has been struck between the prosecutor and the defendant's attorney whereby some form of leniency is promised in exchange for a guilty plea.

Political question. When the courts refuse to rule because they believe that under the U.S. Constitution the founders meant that the matter at hand should be dealt with by Congress or the president.

Private law. This deals with the rights and obligations that private individuals and institutions have when they relate to one another.

Probation. Punishment for a crime that allows the offender to remain in the community and out of jail so long as he or she follows court-ordered guidelines about his or her behavior.

Pro bono publico. ("For the public good.") Usually refers to legal representation undertaken without fee for some charitable or public purpose.

Public law. The relationships that individuals have with the state as a sovereign entity — for example, the tax code, criminal laws, and Social Security legislation.

Recess appointment. An appointment made by the president when Congress is in recess. Persons appointed in this manner may hold office only until Congress reconvenes.

Reversible error. An error committed at the trial court level that is so serious that it requires the appellate court to reverse the decision of the trial judge.

Rule of four. On the Supreme Court at least four justices must agree to take a case before the Court as a whole will consider it.

Rule of 80. When the sum of a federal judge's age and number of years on the bench is 80, Congress permits the individual to retire with full pay and benefits.

Self-restraint (judicial). The reluctance of a judge to inject into a case his or her own personal ideas of what is good or bad public policy. See also activism (judicial).

Senatorial courtesy. Under this practice, senators of the president's political party who object to a candidate that the president wishes to appoint to a district judgeship in their home state have a virtual veto over the nomination.

Sequestration (of jury). In very important or notorious cases the jury may be kept away from the public eye by the judge, and this usually means that the jury is housed and fed as a group at taxpayers' expense.

Socialization (judicial). The process by which a new judge is formally and informally trained to perform the specific tasks of the judgeship.

Standing. The status of someone who wishes to bring a lawsuit. To have standing, the person must have suffered (or be immediately about to suffer) a direct and significant injury.

Stare decisis, the doctrine of. ("Stand by what has been decided.") In effect, the tradition of honoring and following previous decisions of the courts and established points of law.

Statutory law. The type of law enacted by a legislative body, such as Congress, a state legislature, or a city council.

Three-judge panels (of appellate courts). Most decisions of the U.S. courts of appeals are not made by the entire court sitting together but by three judges, often selected at random, to hear any given case.

Three-judge district courts. With some types of important cases Congress has mandated that the case cannot be heard by a U.S. trial judge acting alone but has to be decided by a panel of three judges, one of whom must be an appeals court judge.

Tort. A civil wrong or breach of duty to another person.

Trial de novo. A new trial in which the entire case is retried as if no prior trial had occurred.

Venue. The geographical location in which a case is tried.

Voir dire. The procedure by which opposing attorneys question potential jurors to determine whether the jurors might be prejudicial to their individual cases.

Warrant. Issued after a complaint, filed by one person against another, has been presented and reviewed by a magistrate who has found probable cause for the arrest.

Writ of certiorari. An order issued by the U.S. Supreme Court directing the lower court to transfer records for a case that it will hear on appeal.

Writ of mandamus. A court order compelling a public official to perform his or her duty.

BIBLIOGRAPHY

BOOKS

Administrative Office of the United States Courts. *United States Courts: Their Jurisdiction and Work.* Washington, DC: 1989.

Fallon, Richard H., Hart, Henry Melvin, and Wechsler, Herbert. *Hart and Wechsler's the Federal Courts and the Federal System,* 5th ed. New York, NY: Foundation Press, 2003.

Baum, Lawrence. *American Courts: Process and Policy.* 5th ed. Boston, MA: Houghton Mifflin, 2001.

Chemerinsky, Erwin. *Federal Jurisdiction,* 4th ed. New York, NY: Aspen Publishers, 2003.

Feinman, Jay M. *Law 101: Everything You Need to Know About the American Legal System.* New York, NY: Oxford University Press, Inc., 2000.

Franklin, Carl J. *Constitutional Law for the Criminal Justice Professional.* Boca Raton, FL: CRC Press, 1999.

Friedman, Lawrence Meir. *Law in America: A Short History.* New York, NY: Modern Library, 2002.

Mullenix, Linda S., Martin Redish, and Georgene Vairo. *Understanding Federal Courts and Jurisdiction.* New York, NY: Matthew Bender, 1998.

Posner, Richard A. *The Federal Courts: Challenge and Reform.* Cambridge, MA: Harvard University Press, 1996.

Stumpf, Harry P. *American Judicial Politics,* 2nd ed. Upper Saddle River, NJ: Prentice Hall, 1998.

WEB SITES

Facts About the American Judicial System
http://www.abanet.org/media/factbooks/judifact.pdf

Federal Courts and What They Do
http://www.fjc.gov/public/pdf.nsf/lookup/FCtsWhat.pdf/$file/FCtsWhat.pdf

The Federal Court System in the United States: An Introduction for Judges and Judicial Administrators in Other Countries
http://www.uscourts.gov/library/internationalbook-fedcts2.pdf

InfoUSA — Judicial Branch
http://usinfo.state.gov/usa/infousa/
politics/judbranc.htm

Introduction to the Legal System
http://www.cec.org/pubs_info_
resources/law_treat_agree/summary_
enviro_law/publication/
usdoc.cfm?varlan=english&topic=1

JURIST: The Legal Education
Network
http://www.jurist.law.pitt.edu/

Law Library Resource Exchange
http://www.llrx.com/

Legal Encyclopedia
http://www.nolo.com/lawcenter/ency/
index.cfm

Library of Congress: Guide to Law
Online
http://www.loc.gov/law/guide/us.html

National Center for State Courts —
Court Information Database
http://www.ncsconline.org/WCDS/
index.htm

Prosecutors in State Courts, 2001
http://www.ojp.usdoj.gov/bjs/pub/
pdf/psc01.pdf

State Court Organization, 1998
http://www.ojp.usdoj.gov/bjs/pub/
pdf/sco98.pdf

The Supreme Court of the United
States
http://www.supremecourtus.gov

Understanding the Federal Courts
http://www.uscourts.gov/
understand02/

INDEX

A

Abortion, 173–175
Actus reus, 95
Administrative law, 7, 12, 60
 quasi-judicial bodies, 130, 131
Administrative Procedure Act, 12
Administrative law courts, 39
Advisory opinions, 24, 63, 64, 81
Advocates
 ... *see* Lawyers
Affirmative action, 35, 36
Alternative dispute resolution, 127–131
 arbitration, 128, 129
 mediation, 128
 mini-trial, 129
 neutral fact-finding, 129
 private judging, 130
 summary jury trial, 129, 130
American Bar Association, 145, 147–149
Amicus curiae, 86–89
Anticipatory socialization, 150, 151
Appeals, 116, 117, 139
Appellate courts
 ... *see* Jurisdiction; U. S. Courts of
 Appeal; U. S. Supreme Court
Arbitration, 128, 129
Arraignment, 100, 101
Arrest, 97
Article I, 9, 10, 39
Article II, 144, 149
Article III, 20, 152, 153
 jurisdiction, 9, 24, 25, 63
 courts, creation of, 39, 144
Article IV, 69
Article VI, 7, 8, 16
Articles of Confederation, 7
Assistance of counsel
 ... *see* Counsel, assistance of
Attorneys
 ... *see* Lawyers

B

Bail, 98, 99
Baker v. Carr, 69
Bankruptcy, 122
Bench trial, 106
Bill
 ... *see* Laws
Bill of information, 100
Bill of Rights
 bail, 98, 99
 bills of attainder, 95
 counsel, assistance of, 79, 81–83, 106,
 160, 171–173
 double jeopardy, 58, 101, 106, 114,
 117
 Eighth Amendment, 161
 ex post facto laws, 95
 Fifth Amendment, 13, 58, 99, 106
 First Amendment, 88, 161
 Fourth Amendment, 106
 Miranda rights, 98, 99, 167, 170, 172,
 173
 public trial, 38, 105
 self-incrimination, 106
 Seventh Amendment, 38, 131, 135
 Sixth Amendment, 38, 105
 speedy trial, 98, 99, 105
 Tenth Amendment, 16
 text of, 192–194
 witnesses, confronting, 98, 100, 106,
 108, 109
Bills of attainder, 95
Briefs, 86–89
Brown v. Board of Education, 16, 27, 86,
 160, 165, 169
Burden of proof, 69, 70, 106
 in criminal trial, 112
Burger, Warren, 146, 172

C

Capital punishment, 114, 115, 161
Case citation format, 13, 131
Certified question, 61
Certiorari, writ of, 28, 61
Challenge for cause, 107
Checks and balances, 7
Child custody, 126, 127
Church and state, separation of, 168, 169
Circuit riding, 32
Circuit Court Act of 1802, 32
City courts, 49
Civil law
    adversarial process in, 131
    alternative dispute resolution,
    127–131
    categories of, 121–127
    constitutional rights, 81, 82
    criminal law, comparison to, 15
    damages, 122, 123
    definition of, 120
    federal, 59
    remedies, 14
    standard of proof, 14, 131, 138
    trials, costs of, 127
Civil procedure
    answer, 134
    appeals, 139
    counter claims, 134
    default judgment, 133
    discovery, 134
    filing, 131, 132
    judgment and execution, 138
    jurisdiction, 132
    jury selection, 135, 136
    motions, 133
    peremptory challenges, 135, 136
    pleadings, 133
    post-trial motions, 138
    pretrial conference, 134
    service of process, 133
    standing, 131
    summons, 133
    trial, 136–138

venue, 132, 133
voir dire, 135
Civil Rights Act of 1964, 165, 169
Civil Rights Act of 1968, 62
Clerk of the court, 54, 55
Closing argument, 109, 137
Colonial era
    courts in, 46, 47
    legal profession in, 74
Commerce clause, 9, 10
Commercial law, 121
Common law, 7, 12, 13
Compensatory damages, 122
Compensatory litigation, 83, 84
Concurring opinions, 31
Consensual crime, 94
Constitution
    ... see U. S. Constitution
Constitutional Convention, 20
Constitutional courts, 39
Contract law, 121, 122
Conventional crime
    ... see Crimes of violence; Property
    crime
Counsel, assistance of, 76, 131
    right to, 81-83, 106, 160, 171-172
Counterclaims, 134
County courts, 49
Court unification movement, 48
Courtroom workgroup, 81, 82
Courts
    civil, 130
    conflicts with legislatures, 9, 10, 47
    domestic relations, 130
    jurisdiction, requirements for, 63–71
    probate, 130
    and public policy, 26, 61–71,
    160–163, 168–176
    small claims, 130
    ... see also Federal courts; State courts
Courts of Appeal
    ... see under State Courts,
    intermediate appellate courts
Courts of equity, 15

Creditors' rights, 122
Crime
  actus reus, 95
  consensual, 94
  definition of, 92, 93
  degrees of, 49
    felony, 92, 93
    infractions, 93
    misdemeanors, 93
  domestic violence, 98
  economic, 93, 94
  elements of, 94–96
  homicide, 95, 96
  injury, nature of, 96
  mens rea, 95
  of violence, 93
  organized, 94
  political, 94
  property, 93, 97
  punishment, 92, 93, 102, 114, 115,
    161
Crimes against the person, 93
Crimes of violence, 93
Criminal due process, 170–173
Criminal law, 120
  burden of proof, 69, 70, 106, 112
  capital punishment, 114, 115, 161
  categories of, 92, 93
  civil law, comparison to, 15
  constitutional rights, 81, 82
  federal, 58
  plea bargaining, 79, 82, 101–104
  police discretion, 97, 98
  sentencing, 114–116, 161
  standard of proof, 14, 112
  trials, roles of judges and lawyers, 81,
    82
  ... see also Crime; Defendant's rights;
  Trial
Criminal procedure
  arraignment, 100, 101
  arrest, 97
  assistance of counsel, 106, 160,
    171–173
  bail, 98, 99
  bill of information, 100
  burden of proof, 106
  constitutional rights, 105, 106
  cross examination, 108, 109
  double jeopardy, 114
  due process, 170–173
  exclusionary rule, 106, 170–172
  grand jury, 99, 100
  indictment, 100
  innocence, presumption of, 106
  magistrate, appearance before, 98
  mistrial, 108, 114
  plea bargaining, 79, 82, 101–104
  pleas, 100, 101
  preliminary hearing, 99, 100
  voir dire, 107
  warrant, 97
  ... see also Defendant's rights
Criminal trial
  ... see under Trial
Cross-examination, 108, 109, 136

D
Damages, 122, 123, 138, 139
Davis v. U. S., 173
Death penalty
  ... see Capital punishment
Declaration of Independence, 6
Declaratory judgments, 64
Default judgment, 133
Defendant's rights
  assistance of counsel, 79, 81–83, 106,
    160, 171–173
  bail, 98, 99
  bills of attainder, 95
  Davis v. U. S., 173
  double jeopardy, 58, 101, 106, 114,
    117
  ex post facto laws, 9, 95
  Gideon v. Wainwright, 160, 167,
    170–172, 176
  Harris v. New York, 172, 173
  jury, 38, 105

Mapp v. Ohio, 170–172
Miranda rights, 98, 99, 167, 170, 172, 173
    public trial, 38, 105
    self incrimination, 106
    speedy trial, 98, 99, 105
    trials, 105, 106
    witnesses, confronting, 98, 100, 106, 108, 109
Defendants
    indigent, 76, 79, 81–83
    ... *see also* Counsel, assistance of
Delegation of powers, 8, 9, 12
Depositions, 134
Desegregation
    ... *see* Racial equality
Dicta, 163
Discovery, 134
Dissenting opinions, 31
District Attorney
    ... *see* Prosecutors
Diversity jurisdiction, 9, 10, 59
Divorce, 126, 127
Domestic relations courts, 49, 130
Domestic violence, 98
Double jeopardy, 58, 101, 106, 114, 117

E
Economic crime, 93, 94
Eighth Amendment, 161
Elementary and Secondary Education Act, 165
En banc proceedings, 36
Engel v. Vitale, 168
Equal protection clause, 16, 27, 35, 36
Equitable remedies, 14, 15
Establishment of religion, 64–67
Evarts Act, 32, 33
Evidence, 106, 108, 109, 137
Ex post facto laws, 9, 95
Exclusionary rule, 106, 170–172
Executive branch, 10, 12
    influence on judicial decisions, 165–167

Executive privilege, 165, 166
Exemplary damages, 122
Exhaustion of remedies, 68
Expert witnesses, 136

F
Family law, 125–128
Federal Bureau of Investigation, 10, 145, 147
Federal courts
    administration of, 40–43
    advisory opinions, 63, 64
    chart of, 22
    creation of, 20–22
    jurisdiction of
        diversity, 59
        original, 28, 59–61
    mootness, 63, 64
    standing, 63
    structure of, 20–22
    workload of, 43
    ... *see also* U. S. Courts of Appeal; U. S. District Courts; U. S. Supreme Court
Federal criminal law, 58
Federal Declaratory Judgment Act of 1934, 64
Federal executive branch
    development of, 10, 12
    interaction with judiciary, 10
Federal judges
    ... *see under* Judges
Federal Judgeship Act of 1990, 38
Federal law
    civil law, 59
    components of, 6, 7
    judicial interpretation of, 164
    relationship to state law, 6, 7, 17
    sources of, 7–13
Felonies, 49, 92, 93
Fifth Amendment, 13, 58, 99, 106
First Amendment, 88, 161
Former jeopardy
    ... *see* Double jeopardy

Fourteenth Amendment, 16, 26, 105
  equal protection, 27, 35, 36, 69, 107
Fourth Amendment, 106
Freedom of religion, 86–88
Freedom of speech, 161
Freedom of the press, 47
Friend of the court brief
  ... see Amicus curiae
Frontiero v. Richardson, 166, 167
Furman v. Georgia, 161

G
Gibbons v. Ogden, 26
Gideon v. Wainwright, 160, 167, 170–172, 176
Ginsburg, Ruth, 143
Grand jury, 38, 99, 100
Guilty plea, 101

H
Habeas corpus, 59
Habitual criminal, 102
Harmless error, 116
Harris v. New York, 172, 173
Holmes, Oliver Wendell, 40, 41
Homicide, 95, 96
Hopwood v. Texas, 35, 36
Hung jury, 114

I
Impeachment, 152, 153, 157
Indictment, 58, 100
Indigent defendants, 76, 79, 81–83
Infractions, 49, 93
Innocence, presumption of, 106
Insurance law, 122, 128
Interest groups, 84–89
Interrogatories, 134
Intestate succession, 125

J
Jay, John, 24
Judgment n.o.v., 138
Judgments, 138

Judges
  criminal trial, role in, 81, 82, 104, 105, 109, 111, 112
  decisions
    access to, 161, 162
    Congressional influence on, 163–165, 173
    dicta, 163
    executive branch influence on, 165–167
    implementation of, 166–168
    precedential value of, 160–163
  discretion of, 160, 161
  en banc panels, 36
  federal
    American Bar Association, 147, 149
    anticipatory socialization, 150, 151
    appointment of, 144–150
    disability of, 153
    disciplinary action against, 152
    diversity, 142, 143
    educational background, 142
    impeachment, 152, 153
    and political views, 150, 153
    prebench experience, 142, 143
    qualifications of, 144, 145
    removal of, 152, 153
    Senate Judiciary Committee, 145, 149
    senatorial courtesy, 146, 149
    senior status, 153
    tenure, 151–153, 160
    training, 150, 151
  panels of, 36
  private judging, 130
  state
    appointment of, 155–157
    diversity, 154
    election of, 155, 156
    Missouri Plan, 156
    and political views, 157
    removal of, 157

tenure, 157
tenure, 39, 40, 151–153, 157, 160
terms of, 39, 40
training of, 42, 43, 49, 51
Judgments
    default, 133
    enforcement and implementation of,
    138, 139, 163–168
    impact of, 168–175
    precedential value of, 13, 68, 160–163
Judicial Councils Reform and Judicial
Conduct and Disability Act, 152
Judicial panels, 36
Judicial policy, 61–71, 160–163, 168–176
Judicial precedent, 13, 68, 160–163
Judicial review, 25, 26
Judicial self-restraint, 63–71
Judiciary Act of 1789, 20–22, 25, 32, 37,
39
Jurisdiction
    actual controversy, 63
    appellate, 28
    beneficiaries of law, 67
    burden of proof, 69, 70
    concurrent, 61
    determined by legislature, 62, 63
    diversity, 9, 10, 59
    exhaustion of remedies, 68
    federal, 9-12
    judicial self restraint, 63
    legal versus factual questions, 67, 68
    mootness, 63
    original, 28, 59–61
    personal, 132
    prerequisites to, 63–71
    separation of powers, 68, 69
    specificity of plea, 65, 67
    standing, 63
    state courts, 12, 13
    subject matter, 132
Jury
    challenges, 107, 135, 136
    civil trial
        number of jurors, 135

peremptory challenges, 135, 136
    role in, 136, 138
    selection of jurors, 135
    voir dire, 135
    constitutional issues, 105, 106
    criminal trial
        deliberations, 112 –114
        number of jurors, 107, 108
        role in, 111–114
        selection of jurors, 106, 107, 108
        voir dire, 107
    deadlock, 112–114
    hung, 114
    impartial, 105
    instructions, 112, 137, 138
    number of, 38, 107, 108, 135
    polling, 114, 138
    right to, 38
    sequestration of, 112
    Seventh Amendment, 38
    Sixth Amendment, 38
    summary jury trial, 129, 130
    verdict, 114
    voir dire, 107, 135
    … see also Grand jury
Justice of the peace courts, 49
Justiciability, as prerequisite to
jurisdiction, 63–71
Juvenile courts, 52-53
    age of offenders, 53
    jurisdiction of, 53

L
Land use law, 123–125
Law clerks, 40–42, 53
Law firms, 76, 77
Law schools, 74, 75
Laws
    adoption of, 8, 9
    creation of, 7–9
    education in, 74, 75
    relation of state and federal law, 17
    sources of, 9–13
    U.S. Code, 8, 9

... *see also* Civil law; Criminal law
Lawyers
  criminal trials, role in, 81, 82
  development of the legal profession,
  74, 75
  education of, 74, 75
  government, 78–81
  number of, 76
  pro bono services, 77
  professional opportunities for, 75–81
  professional stratification of, 76–78
  role of, 81
  ... *see also* Prosecutors; Public
  defenders
Legal aid
  ... *see* Counsel, assistance of
Legal Aid societies, 82
Legal profession, 74–78
  ... *see also* Lawyers
Legal remedies, 14, 15
Legislative courts, 39
Legislatures, conflicts with courts, 9, 10,
47
Liens, 139
Litigants, 83, 84
Lucas v. South Carolina Coastal Council,
84

M
Magistrate courts, 49
Magistrates, 53
  appearance before, 98-99
Mandamus, 25
Mandatory sentence, 102, 116
Mapp v. Ohio, 170–173
Marbury v. Madison, 9, 25, 26
Marriage, law of, 125, 126
Marshall, John, 24, 26
Marshall, Thurgood, 86, 143
McCulloch v. Maryland, 26
Mediation, 128
Medical malpractice, 123
Mens rea, 95
Metropolitan courts, 49

Miranda rights
  ... *see under* Defendant's rights
Miranda v. Arizona, 98, 99, 167, 170, 172,
173
Misdemeanors, 49, 93
Missouri Plan, 156
Mistrial, 108, 114, 138
Mootness, 63
Motions
  civil, 133, 137, 138
  post-trial, 115, 138
Municipal courts, 49
Murder, 95, 96

N
Negligence, 122
New Jersey Plan, 20
No-fault divorce, 126
Nolo contendere, 101
Norm enforcement, 38, 39

O
O'Connor, Sandra Day, 143
Obscenity, 161
Opening statements, 108, 136
Opinions, by courts, 30, 31
Oral argument, 29, 30, 36
Organized crime, 94
Original jurisdiction, 28, 59–61

P
Paralegals, 77
Pardons, 116
Penalties
  ... *see* Remedies; Sentencing
Peremptory challenge, 107
Personal injury law, 122
Personal jurisdiction, 132
Personal property, 123
Petit jury, 38
  ...*see* also Jury
Physical evidence, 108
Plea bargaining, 79, 82
  restrictions on, 102, 103

sentencing, 102
  types of, 101, 102
  value of, 103, 104
Pleadings, 133, 134
Pleas, 100, 101
Plessy v. Ferguson, 27
Police, discretion of, 97, 98
Political crime, 94
Political interest groups, 147
Post trial motions, 115
Powell, Lewis F., 42
Precedent
  ...*see* Judicial precedent
Preliminary hearing, 99, 100
Preponderance of the evidence, 14, 131, 138
Private law, 83, 84
Pro bono services, 77
Probable cause, 97
Probate courts, 130
Probation, 115
Product liability law, 122
Property crime, 93, 97
Property law, 123–125
Prosecutors
  federal, 78
  state, 78, 79
Public defenders, 76, 79, 81–83
Public interest law firm, 86
Public law, 83, 84
Public policy and courts, 26, 61–71, 160–163, 168–176
Public trial, 105
Punitive damages, 122

R
Racial equality, 26, 27, 165, 175, 176
  Brown v. Board of Education, 27, 86, 87
  Civil Rights Act of 1968, 62
  equal protection, 62
  Hopwood v. Texas, 35, 36
  Plessy v. Ferguson, 27
  San Antonio Ind. School Dist. v.

  Rodriguez, 62
  separate but equal, 27
  U. S. Supreme Court decisions, 168–170
Real property, 123, 124
Reapportionment, 69
Reasonable doubt, 112
Rebuttal evidence, 109, 137
Recognizance, 99
Rehnquist, William, 173
Remedies, 14, 15, 167
Repeat offender, 102
Roe v. Wade, 173–175
Rules of Criminal Procedure, 103

S
San Antonio Ind. School Dist. v. Rodriguez, 62
Search and seizure, 106
Segregation
  ... *see* Racial equality
Self incrimination, 106
Senate Judiciary Committee, 145, 149
Senatorial courtesy, 146, 149
Senior status, 153
Sentencing
  capital punishment, 114, 115, 161
  concurrent sentence, 102
  guidelines, 115, 116
  mandatory, 102, 116
  pardons, 116
  probation, 115
Separation of powers, 7–11, 21, 68, 69
  executive branch, 10, 11
  judicial branch, 9, 10, 12
  legislative branch, 8, 9
Service of process, 133
Seventh Amendment, 38, 131, 135
Sixth Amendment, 38, 105
Small claims courts, 130
Special scrutiny, 69
Specialized courts, 130
Speedy trial, 105
Speedy Trial Act of 1974, 105

Standard of proof, 14
  in civil courts, 131, 138
  in criminal courts, 112
Standing, 63
Stare decisis, 13
State Attorneys General, 80, 81
State constitutions, 17, 61, 62
  jury trials, 135
State courts
  administration of, 53–55
  caseloads of, 55, 62
  clerk of the court, 54, 55
  courts of last resort (Supreme
    Courts), 49, 51, 52
  development of, 46–48
  family courts, 53
  intermediate appellate courts (courts
    of appeal), 49, 51
  jurisdiction of, 61, 62
  juvenile courts, 52, 53
  law clerks in, 53
  magistrates, 53
  organization of, 46, 48–53
  specialized courts, 48
  trial courts of general jurisdiction, 49,
    51
  trial courts of limited jurisdiction, 48,
    49
State law, relation to federal law, 17
States, powers of under the U. S.
  Constitution, 16
Statutes
  ... *see* Laws
Stipulations, 134
Stone, Harlan Fiske, 41, 146
Strict liability, 122
Subject matter jurisdiction, 132
Succession, law of, 125
Summons, 133
Supremacy clause, 7, 8
Supreme Court
  ... *see* U. S. Supreme Court
Supreme Courts
  ... *see under* State Courts, courts of

  last resort
Syndicated crime
  ... *see* Organized crime

T
Taft, William Howard, 41
Taney, Roger, 26
Tenth Amendment, 16
Tenure
  ... *see under* Judges
Testaments, 125
Thomas, Clarence, 143
Tort law, 122, 123
Trial
  adversarial process, 104, 105
  bench trial, 106
  civil
    adversarial process in, 131
    appeal, 139
    closing arguments, 137
    cross-examination, 136
    discovery, 134
    judgments, 138, 139
    jury, 135–138
    motions, 133, 137
    opening statements, 136
    plaintiff's case, 136
    post-trial motions, 138
    pretrial conference, 134-135
    rebuttal evidence, 137
    standard of proof, 14, 131, 138
    suit, filing of, 131, 132
    testimony, 136, 137
    verdict, 138
    witnesses, 136, 137
  criminal
    appeal, 116, 117
    burden of proof, 69, 70, 106
    closing arguments, 109
    cross-examination, 108, 109
    defendant's case, 109
    errors in, 116
    evidence in, 108, 109
    hung jury, 114

judge, role of, 104, 105, 109–112
jury polling, 114
jury selection, 106, 108
jury, role of, 111, 112
opening statement, 108
post trial motions, 115
prosecution case, 108-109
rebuttal evidence, 109
sentencing, 114–116, 161
standard of proof, 14, 112
verdict, 114
witnesses, confronting, 98, 106
evidence, 108
participants in
lawyers, 81, 82
litigants, 83, 84
summary jury trial, 129, 130
voir dire, 107
Trial courts
... see U. S. District Courts
Trial de novo, 49, 50

U
U. S. Attorney General, 78, 146, 147
U. S. Circuit Courts, 32, 33
U. S. Code, 8, 9
U. S. Congress
advice and consent, 144
influence on judicial decisions, 163–165, 173
powers of, 12, 22
to create courts, 39
under the U. S. Constitution, 8, 9, 144
Senate, 144–147, 149, 150
U. S. Constitution
amendment of, 164, 165
Article I, 9, 10, 39
Article II, 10, 12, 144, 149
Article III, 9, 20, 24, 25, 39, 63, 144, 152, 153
Article IV, 69
Article VI, 7, 8, 16
assistance of counsel, 106, 131,

170–172
bail, 98, 99
bills of attainder, 95
burden of proof, 106
commerce clause, 9, 10
Congress, powers of, 8, 9
delegation of powers, 8, 9, 12
double jeopardy, 101, 106, 114, 117
due process rights, 131
Eighth Amendment, 161
equal protection clause, 16, 62
establishment of religion, 64–67
ex post facto law, 95
exclusionary rule, 106, 170–172
executive branch, 10, 12
federal judiciary, 9, 10
Fifth Amendment, 13, 58, 99, 106
First Amendment, 88, 161
Fourteenth Amendment, 16, 26, 27, 35, 36, 69, 105, 107
Fourth Amendment, 106
freedom of religion, 86-88
freedom of speech, 161
freedom of the press, 47
interpretation of, 164
jury, 38, 105
Miranda rights, 98, 99, 167, 170, 172, 173
obscenity, 161
probable cause, 97
public trial, 105
real property, 125
rights under, 81, 82, 131
search and seizure, 106
self incrimination, 106
separation of church and state, 168, 169
Seventh Amendment, 38, 131, 135
Sixth Amendment, 38, 105
speedy trial, 98, 99, 105
states, 16
Tenth Amendment, 16
text of, 177–203
trials, 105, 106

witnesses, confronting, 98, 100, 106, 108, 109
zoning, 125
... *see also* Bill of Rights; Defendant's rights; Separation of powers
U. S. Court of Military Appeals, 39
U. S. Court of Veterans Appeals, 39
U. S. Court system
creation and structure of, 20–22
... *see also* Federal courts; State courts
U. S. Courts of Appeal, 31–37
appeals
from administrative law tribunals, 60
from U. S. District Courts, 60
caseload of, 43
development of, 32, 33
en banc proceedings, 36
equal protection, 35, 36
geographical boundaries of, 23
hearings before, 36
Hopwood v. Texas, 35, 36
jurisdiction of, 34, 59, 60
law clerks in, 41
opinions in, 36, 37
oral argument in, 36
role of, 34, 35
three judge panels, 36
U. S. Department of Justice, 10, 80, 146, 147, 166
U. S. District Courts
appeals from, 58
caseload of, 43
civil cases in, 58, 59
creation of, 37
criminal cases in, 58
geographical boundaries of, 23
jurisdiction of, 38, 58, 61
law clerks in, 41
organization of, 37, 39
role of, 38, 39
U. S. Attorneys, 78
U. S. Government
federal form of, 22

relationship between branches, 7–13
U. S. Magistrate judges, 40
U. S. Penal Code, 58
U. S. Solicitor General, 78, 80, 89, 166
U. S. Supreme Court
caseload of, 43, 61
cases
Baker v. Carr, 69
Brown v. Board of Education, 27, 86, 87, 160, 165, 169
Davis v. U. S., 173
Engel v. Vitale, 168
Frontiero v. Richardson, 166, 167
Furman v. Georgia, 161
Gibbons v. Ogden, 26
Gideon v. Wainwright, 160, 167, 170–172, 176
Harris v. New York, 172, 173
Lucas v. South Carolina Coastal Council, 84
Mapp v. Ohio, 170–173
Marbury v. Madison, 25, 26
McCulloch v. Maryland, 26
Miranda v. Arizona, 167, 170, 172, 173
Plessy v. Ferguson, 27
Roe v. Wade, 173–175
San Antonio Ind. School Dist. v. Rodriguez, 62
U. S. v. Nixon, 165, 166
Wisconsin v. Yoder, 86–89
certified question, 61
certiorari, 28
conferences in, 30, 31
courtpacking, 166
criminal due process, 170–173
decisions of
impact, 168–175
implementation, 160, 163–168
overturning, 164, 165, 173
development of, 22–26
first justices of, 22, 24
first sitting of, 24
freedom of religion, 86–88

hearings before, 29, 30
issues before, 26, 27, 169-174
Judiciary Act of 1789, 20–22, 25
jurisdiction of, 13, 22, 24–26
   appellate, 27, 61
   concurrent, 61
   original, 27, 60, 61
justices
   appointment of, 143–150, 166
   Burger, Warren, 146, 172
   Ginsburg, Ruth, 143
   Jay, John, 24
   Marshall, John, 24, 26
   Marshall, Thurgood, 86, 143
   O'Connor, Sandra Day, 143
   Powell, Lewis F., 41
   Rehnquist, William, 173
   Stone, Harlan Fiske, 41, 146
   Taft, William Howard, 41
   Taney, Roger, 26
   Thomas, Clarence, 143
   training of, 150, 151
   Warren, Earl, 170
law clerks in, 40–42
opinions
   concurring, 31
   dissenting, 31
   precedential value of, 13, 68, 160-163
   writing of, 24, 25
oral argument before, 29, 30
racial equality, decisions concerning, 27, 62, 86, 87, 160, 165, 168–170
right to counsel, 170–172
role of, 27, 28
scrutiny, standards of, 69
sessions of, 28, 29
… *see also* Defendant's rights
U. S. Tax Court, 39
U. S. v. Nixon, 165, 166

V
Venue, 132, 133
Verdict, 114, 138

Virginia Plan, 20
Voir dire, 107, 135

W
Warrant, arrest, 97
Warren, Earl, 170
Watergate affair, 165, 166
Wills and estates, 125
Wisconsin v. Yoder, 86–89
Witnesses
   confronting, 98, 106
   cross-examination, 108, 109, 136, 137
Workload of courts, 43, 55, 61, 62
Writs
   certiorari, 28, 61
   habeas corpus, 59
   mandamus, 25

Z
Zoning, 123–125

ACKNOWLEDGMENT

Outline of the American Legal System is a publication of
the United States Department of State. Chapters 1 through 8 are
adapted with permission from the book *Judicial Process in America*,
5th edition, by Robert A. Carp and Ronald Stidham,
published by Congressional Quarterly, Inc.

Picture Credits

Executive Editor: **George Clack**

Managing Editors: **Rosalie Targonski,**
                  Mildred Solá Neely

Art Director/Design: **Min-Chih Yao**

Cover Illustration: **Sally Vitsky**

Photo Research: **Maggie Johnson Sliker**